The Ritual of the Temple in the Time of Christ

Leen & Kathleen Ritmeyer

The Ritual of the Temple in the Time of Christ

Carta, Jerusalem

Illustrations by Leen Ritmeyer
Illustrations on pp. 31 (top), 41 by Carta, Jerusalem
Photograph on p. 62 by Amihai Mazar
Photograph on p. 65 by Michael Luddeni
All photographs of the model by Philip Evans

First edition 2002

Designed and produced by Carta, Jerusalem
Editor: Barbara Ball
Artwork: Leen Ritmeyer
Graphics: Vladimir Shestakovsky

Carta, The Israel Map and Publishing Company Ltd.
18 Ha'uman Street, P.O. Box 2500, Jerusalem 91024
E-mail: cartaben@netvision.net.il
Website: http://holyland-jerusalem.com/

ISBN 965-220-452-8

Printed in Israel

Contents

Introduction

Information on the worship and ritual of Herod's Temple is available in abundance from the Mishnah, the oldest codification of Jewish Law that has come down to us. The Mishnah was compiled at the end of the second century A.D., but there is evidence that some rabbis quoted as authorities lived in the first century and so had known the Temple and all its arrangements before its destruction in A.D. 70. The major source for the description of the Temple is *Middot* (or "Measurements"), one of the oldest tractates of the Mishnah. This tractate has been ascribed to Rabbi Eliezer Ben Jacob, who lived during the final years of the Second Temple period.

The classic work of Alfred Edersheim, *The Temple, its Ministry and Services as they were at the time of Christ*, first published in 1874, is largely based on the Mishnah, although material is also derived from the New Testament, Josephus the contemporary Jewish historian, and Philo, the Greek philosopher. Edersheim had that rare ability of being able to combine commanding vision of a period with the sharpness of observation necessary for its full evocation. We have therefore decided to use the same order employed by Edersheim, following his unrolling of the first-century scene from a first view of Jerusalem and the Temple to the offering of firstfruits in the Temple.

Edersheim employed both Holy Scripture and authoritative ancient sources to construct a work full of revealing insights. The study of how the Law of Moses was observed in the first century A.D. illuminates for us the details and sequence of the Gospel narratives and the prevailing sentiments of the age in which they were written.

The views of the Temple are based on two recently constructed architectural models. The model of Herod's Temple Mount was built to a scale of 1:275, while a scale of 1:75 was used for the model of the Temple proper. Figures and scenes portrayed on the model are true to scale.

About Alfred Edersheim

Alfred Edersheim was born in Vienna in 1825 and attended university there. He then studied Theology at New College, Edinburgh, and later at the University of Berlin. He entered the Presbyterian ministry at the age of 21. He was Grinfield Lecturer in the Septuagint at the University of Oxford from 1884 until his death in 1889. Of Jewish extraction, Edersheim's knowledge of Hebrew and of the Jewish sources, e.g., the Mishnah and Talmud, are much in evidence in his writings.

His other works, apart from the one mentioned above, include *The Life and Times of Jesus the Messiah*, *Sketches of Jewish Social Life in the Days of Christ*, and *Bible History: Old Testament*.

Jerusalem in the time of King Herod.

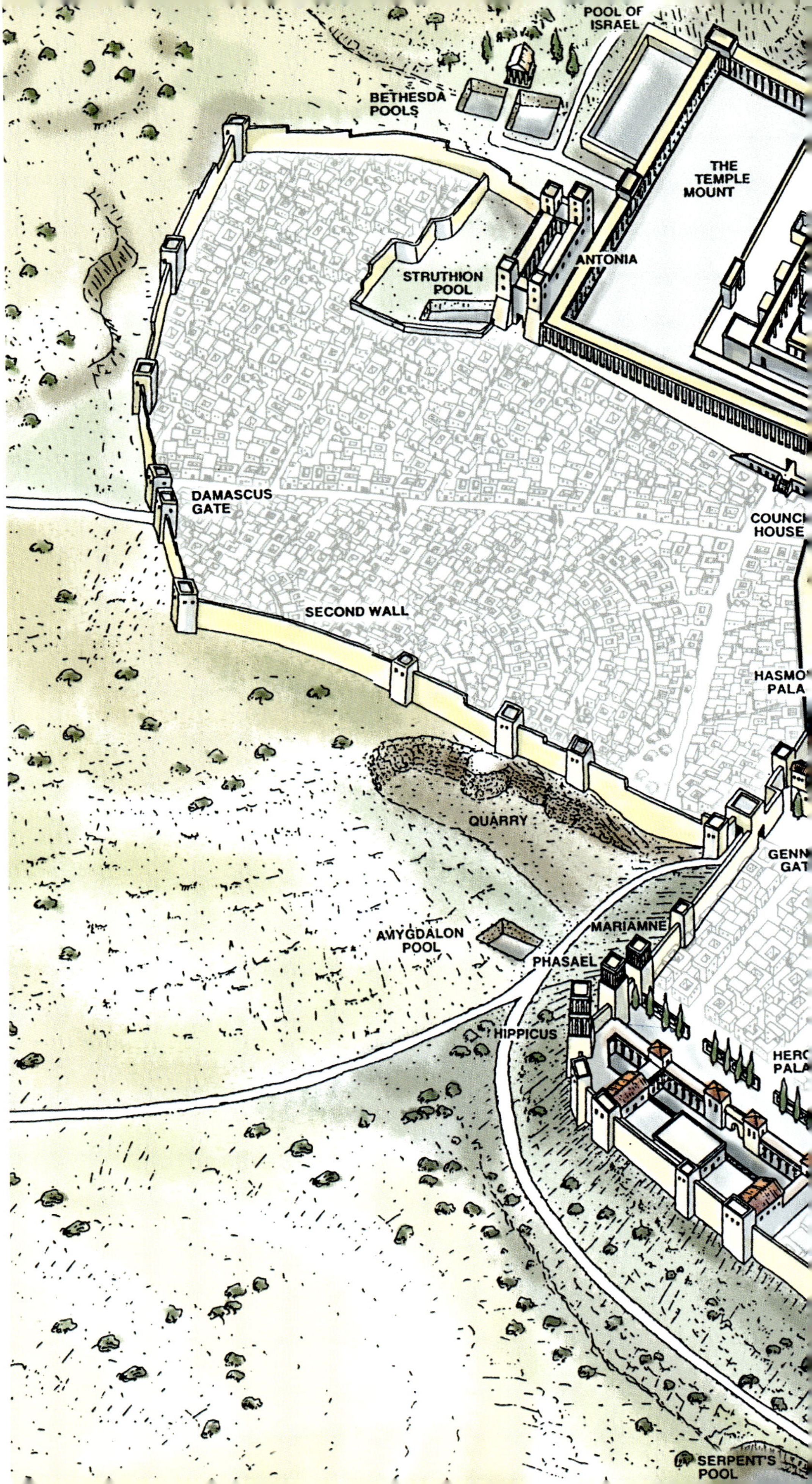

MOUNT
OF OLIVES
KEDRON VALLEY
'THE TOWER THAT
LIETH OUT'
PALACES
OPHEL
'HASMONEAN
TOWER'
PALATIAL
MANSION
TYROPOEON
VALLEY
FIRST WALL
SILOAM
POOL
DAM
DWELLING
GATE
MONUMENT
OF ANNAS
HOUSE OF
CAIPHAS
ST WALL
ESSENES
GATE
HINNOM VALLEY

The Temple Platform

This view of the Temple platform lays the foundation for all the rest. It shows a model of the vast esplanade of the Temple Mount built by King Herod the Great in Jerusalem in the first century A.D. Herod had reconstructed the Temple that was originally built by King Solomon in the tenth century B.C. and destroyed by the Babylonians in 586 B.C. An earlier reconstruction of the Temple, made by the Jewish exiles on their return from Babylon, was named the Second Temple. However, this was considered inferior to the First Temple and so King Herod persuaded the Jewish authorities to allow him to restore it to the magnificence of the Solomonic prototype. Herod's restored Temple Mount thus retained the name "Second Temple."

Like Edersheim, we want to be able to "know exactly how the Temple looked and to find our way through its gates, porches, courts and chambers; to be present if only in spirit at its services; to witness the Morning and Evening sacrifice; to mingle with the crowd of worshippers at the great Festivals, and to stand by the side of those who offered sacrifice or freewill offering, or who awaited the solemn purification which would restore them to the fellowship of the Sanctuary." (Alfred Edersheim, *The Temple, its Ministry and Services as they were at the time of Christ*, London, The Religious Tract Society, 1874, pp. 5–6).

An overall view from the east of the Temple platform as seen from the Mount of Olives. Four gates give access from the west, where the city is located. The two gates on the south, the Double and Triple Gates, are on the left. The Shushan Gate on the east lies opposite the Temple and there is another gate in the south-east. A gate, known as the Tadi Gate, is to the north. The Temple was surrounded by courts with ascending degrees of sanctity. The first barrier, seen on the left, marked the border where one entered into the area considered Holy, the area of the Temple platform that existed before King Herod enlarged it. The low balustrade broken up by narrow entrances was known as the Soreg and this marked the barrier beyond which Gentiles were not allowed to pass.

The Royal Porch or Stoa

Model of the Herodian Temple Mount, showing the Royal Porch or Stoa running along its southern wall. The stoa was built on a basilical plan, with 162 pillars in four rows to divide it into a central nave and two aisles. Each pillar stood 50 feet high. Josephus wrote in his Antiquities *(15.413) that their circumference was such that three men might encircle them with their arms outstretched and touching. Pillars found in the debris of the excavations conform exactly to such a stipulation!*

Edersheim leads us into the Temple via the Royal Porch or Stoa. It could be entered from outside the Temple platform via the monumental staircase that led up from the Tyropoeon Valley. Like most researchers of his time, Edersheim describes a bridge rather than the monumental staircase which was discovered in the excavations that took place here following the 1967 Six Day War. The view, however, would not have been affected by the nature of this structure. "Here the city would have lain spread before us like a map. Beyond it the eye would wander over straggling suburbs, orchards and many gardens—fairest among them the royal gardens to the south, the 'garden of roses,' so celebrated by the Rabbis—till the horizon was bounded by the hazy outline of mountains in the distance" (p. 20).

At the eastern end of the Royal Stoa, the bottom of the Kedron Valley lies some 240 feet (73 m) below. Because of this vast drop, many scholars locate the pinnacle of the Temple, to which Jesus was transported in his imagination by the temptor, at the southeastern corner of the Royal Porch or Stoa (Matt. 4.5, Luke 4.5).

The Court of the Gentiles, located between the Temple and the Royal Stoa and visible here in front of the Stoa, was open to all visitors to the Temple. Edersheim suggests that it was here that Jesus overturned the tables of the moneychangers and those that sold doves (Matt. 21.1–16). However, since the Court of the Gentiles was not part of the sacred area, it is likely that these activities had, on that occasion, spilled over into the hallowed area of the pre-Herodian Temple Mount, thereby provoking Jesus into a confrontation.

The Temple Plan

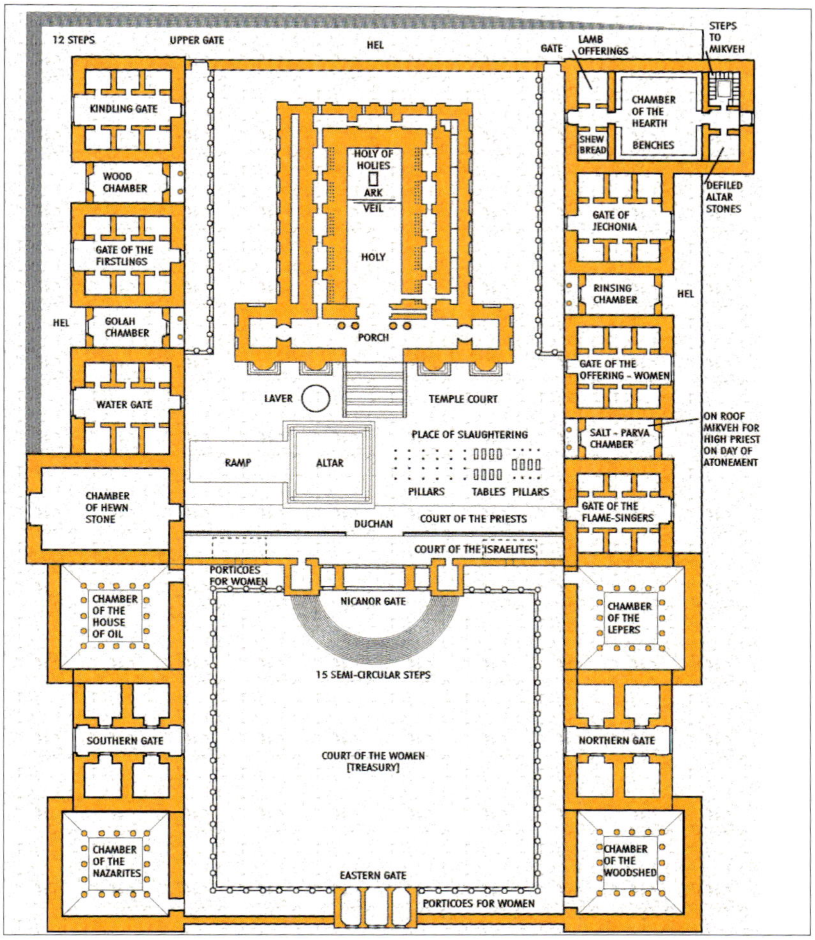

Plan of the Temple Court and the Court of the Women, and the complex of chambers which surrounded the Temple, all based on the specifications given in the Mishnaic tractate, Middot.

This plan is the key to understanding the Temple layout. Beyond the enclosure bordered by the Soreg, a flight of twelve steps, according to the Mishnaic tractate, *Middot* 2.3 (Edersheim believes there were fourteen, but, based on the author's measurements, twelve seems to be correct) led up to a terrace known as the *Hel*, which bordered the Temple on the south and west.

Edersheim sets the scene thus: "We are now approaching the Sanctuary itself, which consisted, first, of three courts, each higher than the former, and beyond them, of the Holy and Most Holy Places with their outbuildings" (p. 24). He describes how one may enter via the Eastern Gate, first into the Court of the Women or Treasury. From there one could advance into the Court of Israel and then into the Court of the Priests. However, he points out that there was a nearer way into the Court of the Priests; via the three gates located on the north and south sides of the Temple. A southern and a northern gate also led into the Court of the Women.

Edersheim identifies the ninth or Eastern gate to the Temple as the Nicanor Gate, as *Middot* 1.4 mentions this gate as being on the east. However, from the description of the gate of Corinthian bronze given in Josephus' *The Jewish War* (5.201), and located just "outside the sanctuary," it is clear that this is synonymous with the Nicanor Gate and that it was the gate that led from the Court of the Women into the Court of the Priests. Edersheim locates the healing of the lame man at what Scripture calls the Beautiful Gate (Acts 2.10) at this same Nicanor Gate. This is because the Nicanor Gate is described in superlatives by Josephus, so Edersheim connects the two.

However, the Eastern Gate of the Temple is the more likely site for this miracle and would correspond with Edersheim's modern-day analogy, "just as privileged beggars now lie at the entrance to continental cathedrals" (p. 25). It is unlikely that beggars would have been allowed to lie on the fifteen semi-circular steps that led into the Court of the Priests while it may well have been permitted to do so at the Eastern Gate leading into the Court of the Women.

The Court of the Women

The Court of the Women was so called not because its use was solely reserved for women, but because this was the farthest they were allowed to proceed into the Temple. In fact, as Edersheim notes, "this was probably the common place for worship, the females occupying, according to Jewish tradition, only a raised gallery along three sides of the court" (p. 26). The Jewish tradition he refers to appears in Middot *2.5, which states that "Beforetime the Court of the Women was free of buildings, and afterward they surrounded it with a gallery, so that the women should behold from above and the men from below and that they should not mingle together." These galleries with their female figures are visible in the foreground. They are also mentioned in the Mishnaic tractate,* Sukkah *5.2, which deals with the laws concerning the Feast of Tabernacles (Succot). Here, too, is explained the significance of the four great lampstands that stood in the Court of the Women.*

The Court of the Women, which Edersheim determines from the Mishnaic measurements as having been 200 feet square (it actually measured 135 cubits square, which, according to the cubit of 20.67 inches, is 230 feet square; this gives a surface of 52,900 sq. feet or 5,023 sq. m), was also known as the Treasury. Israelite men, could, of course, proceed through the Nicanor Gate into the Court of the Israelites.

The Treasury

The thirteen trumpet-shaped boxes for monetary offerings which were placed under the colonnade that encircled the Court of the Women can almost certainly be identified as the Treasury mentioned in Luke (21.1–4) and, as Edersheim writes, "it was probably into one of these that the poor widow dropped her two mites" (p. 26, n. 1).

The Mishnaic tractate, *Shekalim*, which deals with the Shekel dues, records that each of the thirteen chests (or *Shopharot*) carried an inscription indicating the object of the offering. There were receptacles for "New Shekel Dues"; "Old Shekel Dues"; "Bird Offerings"; "Young birds for the whole-offering"; "Wood"; "Frankincense"; and "Gold for the Mercy-seat." The remaining six were for "Freewill-offerings"—one of these would have received what "she of her penury hath cast in all the living that she had."

Edersheim notes that "It is probably in ironical allusion to the form and name of these treasure-chests that the Lord, making use of the word 'trumpet,' describes the conduct of those who, in their almsgiving, sought glory from men as 'sounding a trumpet' before them—that is, carrying before them, as it were, in full display one of these trumpet-shaped alms-boxes" (p. 27).

Two of the thirteen trumpet-shaped receptacles for monetary offerings placed under the colonnade which encircled the Court of the Women.

Chambers in the Court of the Women

In its description of the Court of the Women and its chambers, the tractate *Middot* 2.5 makes a fascinating reference to Ezekiel 46.22, which also describes a court at each of the corners of the Temple Court and deduces "and so shall they be thereafter."

These were unroofed chambers (apart from having roofed porticoes), each 40 cubits or 68 feet (21 m) across, according to Edersheim. The Chamber of the Nazarites, on the southeast, was where those who had taken the vow of the Nazarite cooked their peace-offerings, cut off their hair which had grown for the duration of their vow, and thrown it on the fire under a pot.

The Chamber of the House of Oil is where oil and wine for the drink-offerings were stored. Northwest of the Court of the Women is the Chamber of the Lepers, where those healed of leprosy came to be immersed before presenting themselves before the priest.

In the northeast is the Chamber of the Woodshed, where priests who, because of some blemish, could not take part in the sacrificial service of the Temple, examined the wood destined for use on the Altar. *Shekalim* 6.1 records a Jewish tradition that it was under this chamber that the Ark of the Covenant had been hidden to preserve it from the threat of discovery by enemies of the Jews.

Fifteen semi-circular steps led up to the Nicanor Gate, on the north side of the Court of the Women. Edersheim points out that it was in the Gate of Nicanor that "All that was ordered to be done 'before the Lord' took place. There the cleansed leper and the women coming for purification presented themselves to the priests and there also the 'water of jealousy' was given to the suspected wife" (p. 28).

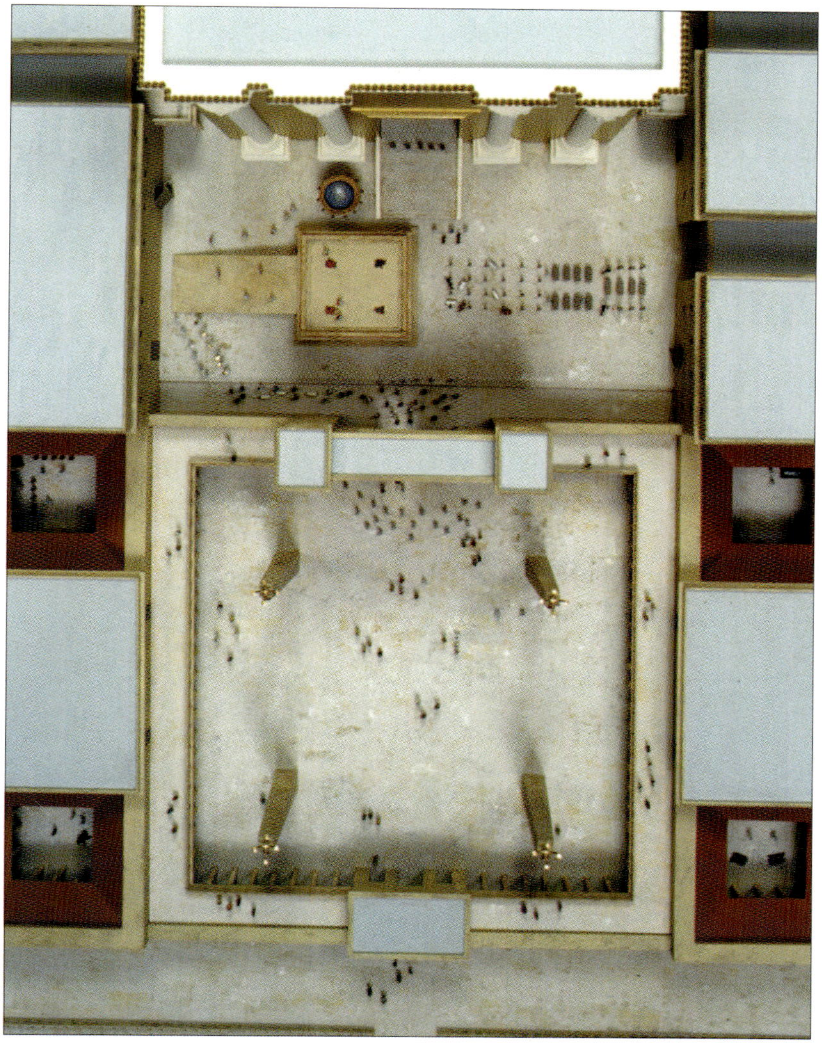

Bird's-eye view of the Temple and surrounding courts. Clearly visible are the chambers, identified by the red roofs, at the four corners of the Court of the Women.

Clockwise, from bottom left, is the Chamber of the Nazarites, with a pot on the right and a Nazarite figure on the left with two priests facing him; the Chamber of the House of Oil, with a row of pots for storing the liquids; the Chamber of the Lepers, showing the bath where the leper was cleansed; the Chamber of the Woodshed, with two piles of wood—one pile deemed fit for use, the other pile worm-eaten and therefore rejected.

Fifteen semi-circular steps, leading up to the Nicanor Gate, are visible on the north side of the Court of the Women. On the other side of the gate lay the Court of the Israelites and the Court of the Priests.

The Court of the Israelites, the Court of the Priests and the Temple Court

The Courts of the Israelites, the Priests and the Temple Court were the closest courts to the Temple. As their level rose in height, so did their sanctity, until one reached the Holy of Holies. The Court of the Israelites was a narrow strip, only 11 cubits (19 ft., 5.8 m) wide. Purified Israelite men, shown here wearing brightly colored clothes, could come into this court to view the ritual of the Temple Court. Edersheim calls this the Court of Israel.

Separating the Court of the Israelites from the Court of the Priests was a step, 1 cubit (20.67 inches, 0.53 m) in height, on which there was a platform (or *Duchan*). On both sides of the *Duchan* were three steps, each half a cubit high. Thus the Court of the Priests was 2.5 cubits (4.3 ft., 1.3 m) higher than the Court of the Israelites and it was 11 cubits (19 ft., 5.8 m.) wide. The Levites used to sing psalms on the *Duchan* during the daily service. Six Levites are shown here wearing white robes and facing the Court of the Israelites.

The scene portrayed by the Israelite figures in colored robes and the priests at the top left is part of the Passover ritual (see p. 49).

In a deviation from pattern, there was no change in level between the Court of the Priests and the Temple Court proper. The latter court was the site of the Laver, the Shambles where the animals were prepared for sacrifice, and the Great Altar of Burnt Sacrifice.

Just west of the Altar were the twelve steps which led up to the Temple Porch, where the priests would pronounce the blessing of Numbers 6.24–26.

The Chambers on the North Side of the Temple

According to *Middot* 1.4, there were three gates on the north side of the Temple Court, three in the south and one in the east. In the north, from east to west, are the Gate of the Flame, the Gate of the Offering and the Chamber of the Hearth which also had a gate. In *Middot* 2.6, the gates in the north are called the Gate of the Singers, the Gate of the Women and the Gate of Jeconiah. As these gates had many chambers in which different activities took place, the same gate may have been ascribed different names.

Middot 5.3 mentions three offices in the north: one contained the salt for the offerings, one was used for the preservation of hides by salting (*Parva* Chamber) and one for the rinsing of the intestines of the sacrificial animals (Rinsing Chamber). A passage led up from the *Parva* Chamber to a chamber located above the middle office, where the High Priest immersed himself on the Day of Atonement. These rooms were probably located in the two spaces left between the three gates. One room may have been positioned above the other. With salt in constant demand, the salt chamber must have been located close to the *Parva* chamber for preparing the hides (see plan, p. 13).

The Chamber of the Hearth (*Beth ha-Moked*), on the right, extends into the northern court. As *Middot* puts it (1.6), "there were four rooms in the Chamber of the Hearth like cells opening into a hall, two within holy ground and two outside holy ground." In other

(opposite) The Court of the Israelites, the Court of the Priests and the Temple Court.

The chambers on the north side of the Temple.

words, the portion of this building that extended beyond the line of the *Hel* was not considered holy. One of the rooms stored the altar-stones which the Syrian kings had defiled, while the other had steps leading down to an underground *mikveh* or ritual bath. Of the two chambers within the *Hel*, that in the southwest was used to keep the lambs in readiness for the daily sacrifices, and that in the southeast was used to make the shewbread. The building was known as the Chamber of the Hearth because of the fires that were kept burning there continually to warm the priests who ministered barefoot.

On the south side of the Temple Court, there was a parallel arrangement of gatehouses. These were, from east to west, the Water Gate, the Gate of the Firstlings and the Kindling Gate. In between these gatehouses was the *Golah* (or Exile) Chamber, where water was drawn from a cistern beneath, and a Wood Chamber. *Middot* also mentions another building, on the south side of the Temple Court, which was vital for the organization of the Temple. This was known as the Chamber of Hewn Stone (*Lishkat ha-Gazit*) and was the site of the convening of the Sanhedrin, the supreme Jewish legislative, religious, and judicial body for judgment. Edersheim notes that "it ought to be remarked that about the time of Christ the Sanhedrin removed its sittings from the Hall of Square Stones (*sic*) to another on the east of the Temple-court" (p. 53, n.1, 54).

The Temple

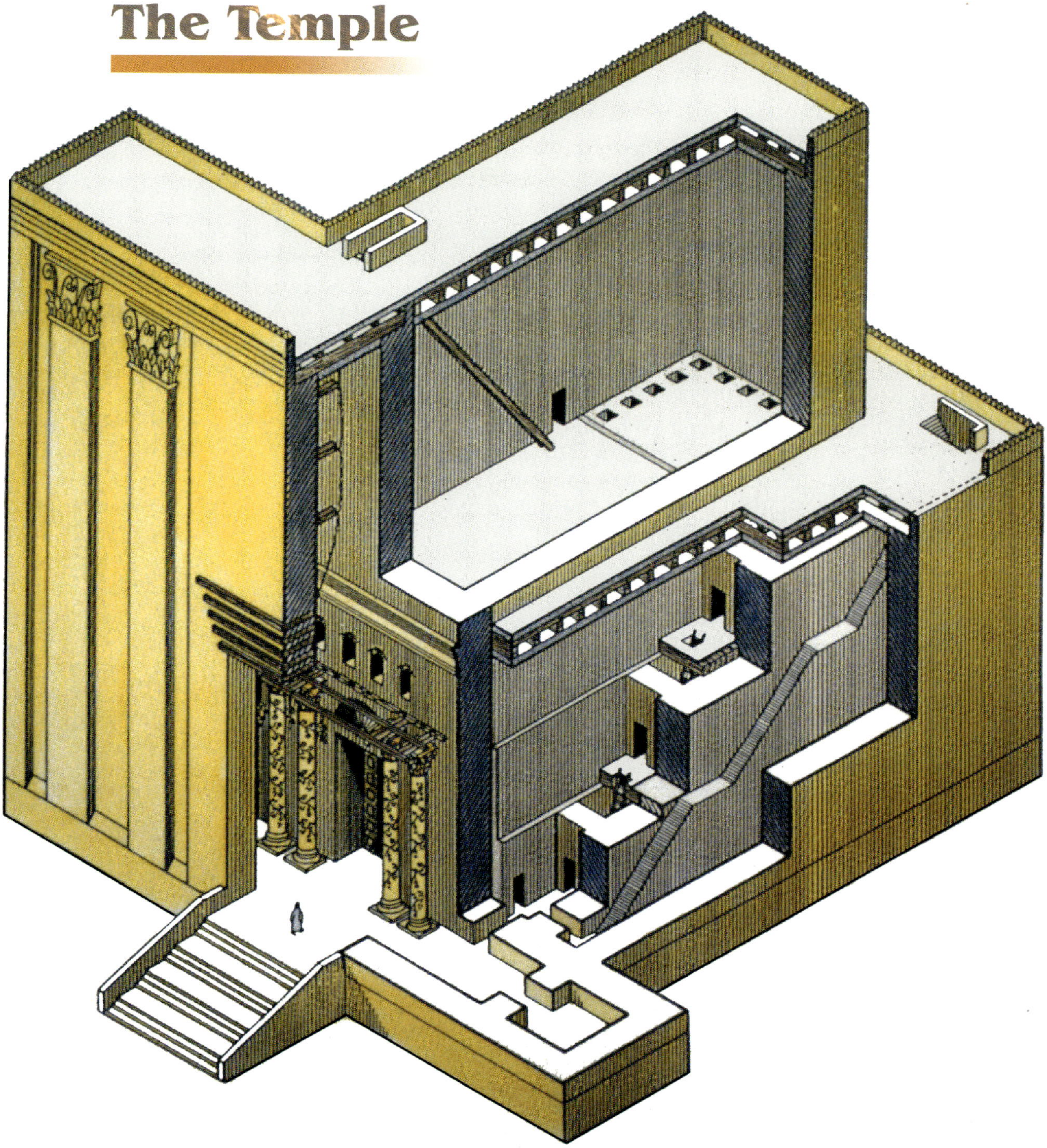

The five oak beams over the entrance to the Temple Porch are clearly visible in this cutaway view. The façade has been removed so that the four columns over which the Golden Vine wreathed can be seen.

This view also makes it possible to appreciate the description of the Temple in Middot *4.7 as "like to a lion . . . narrow behind and wide in front." The writer of the Mishnaic tractate makes the comparison with Ariel, one of the biblical titles of Jerusalem, meaning "Lion of God." The Temple itself was only 70 cubits (120 ft., 36.75 m) wide and 78 cubits (134 ft., 40.95 m) long. Three storeys of cells surrounded the Temple proper which was divided into the Holy Place and the Holy of Holies. Above these stood an Upper Chamber, which had a device for lowering baskets into the Holy of Holies for maintenance purposes and a ladder in the form of two cedar beams with steps cut into them, to reach the upper roof.*

The Temple Facade

The porch of the facade of Herod's Temple. The entrance to the porch was 40 cubits (69 ft., 21 m) high and 20 cubits (34.4 ft., 10.5 m) wide. Above it, five oak beams covered with gold and of graduated length were set in the facade. Beneath these and framing the entrance into the Sanctuary was, as Edersheim puts it, "that symbol of Israel," a vine made of pure gold. A parapet of golden spikes bordered the rooftops to stop birds from soiling the Temple walls.

The porch in front of the magnificent facade of Herod's Temple extended 15 cubits (26 ft., 7.88 m) on either side of the Temple. The porch stood 100 cubits (172 ft., 52.5 m) high and was equally wide. A modern-day parallel in terms of size would be an 18-storey building towering above the surrounding landscape. *Middot* 4.1 records that all the house was overlaid with gold. In this model the facade is ornamented with four columns in the Corinthian style, as depicted on ancient coins.

Combining the descriptions in *Middot* and Josephus' writings, we get a glowing picture of the Temple. Josephus, in his *The Jewish War* (5.222, 223), supplies the following details: "The exterior of the building wanted nothing that could astound either mind or eye. For being covered on all sides with massive plates of gold, the sun was no sooner up than it radiated so fiery a flash that persons straining to look at it were compelled to avert their eyes, as from the solar rays. To approaching strangers it appeared from a distance like a snow-clad mountain; for all that was not overlaid with gold was of purest white."

The Golden Vine

The Golden Vine was one of the most remarkable features in all the Temple precincts. Middot *3.8 records that "A golden vine stood over the entrance to the sanctuary, trained over posts; and whosoever gave a leaf, or a berry, or a cluster as a freewill-offering, he brought it and the priests hung it thereon." Josephus in his* The Jewish War *(5.210) writes that the Temple entrance had "above it those golden vines from which depended grape-clusters as tall as a man."*

This great symbol of the nation may have been used by Jesus in one of his discourses to his disciples. Dean Farrar, who wrote The Life of Christ *at about the same time as Edersheim wrote his great work, suggests that Christ may have been alluding to this very feature of the Temple when he said in John 15.1: "I am the true vine."*

The fame of this vine was such that mention was made of it by non-Jewish writers such as Tacitus and Florus in their descriptions of the taking of Jerusalem by Pompey in 63 B.C.

The priests standing in front of the Golden Vine are reciting the Priestly Blessing.

The Holy Place

*The Holy Place (*ha-Kodesh*) measured 40 cubits (69 ft., 21 m) high and 20 cubits (34.4 ft., 10.50 m) wide. It contained the seven-branched Lampstand (*Menorah*) in the south, the Table of Shewbread (*ha-Shulchan*) in the north, and close to the Veil (*ha-Paroketh*) that separated the Holy Place from the Holy of Holies (*Kodesh ha-Kodashim *or* Debir*), the Altar of Incense (*Mizbe'ach ha-Ketoreth*).*

The specifications for the Lampstand were first laid down in Exodus 25.31, with the original one used in the Tabernacle made of a talent (about the weight of a man) of pure gold. Its design consisted of a central stem with three branches on either side. Each branch had three sets of almond-shaped bowls, buds and flowers. The central stem had four sets of bowls, buds and flowers. There was a golden lamp or oil-cup on top of the stem and each branch. Pure olive oil was used to produce the light. It would appear that since the time that the prototype was crafted, a number of lampstands had been made. In Solomon's Temple, there were ten lampstands in the Holy Place (1 Kings 7.49) and the Lampstand depicted on the Arch of Titus in Rome, celebrating the spoiled Temple treasures in A.D. 70, is markedly different from biblical specifications.

The Table of Shewbread was made of gold-covered shittim wood and measured 2 cubits (3.4 ft., 1.05 m) long by 1 cubit (20.67 inches, 0.52 m) wide and 1.5 cubits (1.7 ft., 0.79 m) high. A gold crown surrounded it on top and it was transported by means of staves that were inserted into gold rings attached to its four legs. Two piles containing six cakes of bread each were placed on the Table of Shewbread and changed by the priests every Sabbath day. Leviticus 24.5–9 stipulates that pure frankincense be put on top of each of the piles of bread.

The Incense Altar was also made of shittim wood and overlaid with gold. It measured 1 cubit (20.67 inches, 0.52 m) square and was 2 cubits (3.4 ft., 1.05 m) high. Exodus 30.1–10 describes it as having horns on each of its corners. It too was carried by staves.

The Veil

The Veil, which separated the Holy from the Holy of Holies in the Second Temple, differed from that described in Exodus 26.31–33. Whereas the latter was made of "blue, and purple, and scarlet, and fine twined linen of cunning work" and decorated with cherubim (or winged creatures), the Veil in Herod's Temple is described as having the symbols of lions and eagles portrayed on it. As there were two of the faces of the cherubim described in Ezekiel 1.10, we have added the remaining two—man and ox.

The Mishnaic tractate Shekalim *8.5 records that the Veil was "one handbreadth thick and was woven on (a loom having) 72 rods, and over each rod were twenty-four threads. Its length was forty cubits and its breadth twenty cubits; it was made by eighty-two young girls and they used to make two in every year." It in fact comprised two curtains with a space between them.*

*On the Day of Atonement, the High Priest entering the Holy of Holies is described as going in via the south side of the slightly open outer curtain, passing between this and an inner curtain, and entering the Holy of Holies on the opposite side, which again was slightly open (*Yoma *5.1). The cubit space between the two curtains was known as "*Amah traqsin*."*

The interior of the Holy of Holies. Here, the High Priest is shown placing his incense censer or fire-pan in the rectangular depression which marked the original emplacement of the Ark of the Covenant. The wall decoration consists of gold sheets and engravings of palmettes.

The priests who did maintenance work in the Holy of Holies were lowered down from the Upper Chamber in a cage that hung against the wall.

The Holy of Holies

The interior of the Holy of Holies was 20 cubits (34.4 ft., 10.50 m) square and 40 cubits (69 ft., 21 m) high. Edersheim writes of Herod's Temple: "The latter was now quite empty, a large stone, on which the High Priest sprinkled the blood on the Day of Atonement, occupying the place where the ark with the mercy-seat had stood" (p. 36). The Ark of the Covenant, which unlike the seven-branched Lampstand could not be reproduced, had been lost or hidden. The last mention of it in history was during the reign of King Josiah (639–608 B.C.), as recorded in 2 Chronicles 35.3. Edersheim derives his "large stone" from the record in *Yoma* 5.2: "After the Ark was taken away a stone remained there from the time of the early Prophets, and it was called *Shetiyah*. It was higher than the ground by three fingerbreadths."

This "foundation stone" has recently been identified as part of the author's research into the development of the Temple Mount throughout its history (Leen Ritmeyer, *The Temple and the Rock*, Harrogate, 1996). The rocky summit of Mount Moriah, on which the Holy of Holies of Solomon's Temple was built, remained slightly higher than the floor of the Temple subsequently built by King Herod on a six-cubit-high foundation. This original stone surface, now known by its Arabic name, the "Sakhra," and enshrined within the Islamic shrine of the Dome of the Rock on the Temple Mount, is a link to the original Temple.

The maintenance of the Holy of Holies was carried out by means of openings around the floor of the Upper Chamber of the Temple. *Middot* 4.5 tells us that "in the upper story were openings into the Holy of Holies by which they used to let down the workmen in boxes, so that they should not feast their eyes on the Holy of Holies."

The system would have worked something like this. A winch would have let a priest down into the Holy of Holies in a basket or cage like the one shown here. These baskets were closed on three sides to prevent the priest from looking inside the Holy of Holies. Maintenance of the Holy of Holies must have required rigorous planning, with the priests being let down systematically through the openings (*lulin*) until all the required work had been accomplished.

Winch and basket system for maintenance of the Holy of Holies.

The Half-shekel Temple Tribute

After setting the scene in describing the Temple, Edersheim passes on to a chapter called Temple Order, Revenues and Music. In this chapter he recalls that the Rabbis lamented the fact that the real elements of Temple glory, the Ark, the holy fire and the *Shechinah* (the divine presence) had left the Temple.

Despite this, deep reverence was enjoined on pilgrims to the Temple, which Edersheim believed might have accommodated 210,000 visitors at a time. He then goes on to speak of the tremendous wealth this throng of people must have brought to the Temple. The Temple treasury was filled by means of money paid with vows or free gifts. Some individuals left their entire fortune to the Temple. Edersheim points out that it may have been to this practice that Christ referred "in denouncing the Scribes and Pharisees who 'devour widows' houses and for a pretence make long prayers' (Matt. 23.14)" (p. 47).

Voluntary offerings were made on the Sabbaths and feast-days, and the meat offerings prepared by the Levites were sold daily to those who needed them for their offerings. There were numerous other instances where Israelites and visitors to the Temple enriched its coffers. The coinage in general usage in this period was minted in Tyre. The Mishnaic tractate *Bekhoroth* 8.7 enumerates some offerings that had to be paid for in Tyrian coinage. These coins, however, were offensive to religious Jews because they have the image of Melkart (who was surnamed Hercules) and could be changed into the shekel of the Sanctuary. A half-shekel of Temple tribute had to be paid by male Israelites over the age of twenty.

Substantial profit was made by the money-changers on every transaction. Edersheim points out that "It must therefore have been a very powerful interest which Jesus attacked, when in the court of the Temple He 'poured out the changers' money, and overthrew the tables,' while at the same time He placed himself in direct conflict with the sanctioned arrangements of the Sanhedrin, whom He virtually charged with profanity" (p. 72).

A Tyrian silver, two-drachma coin which was the equivalent of half a shekel.

Trumpet players in the Temple service. According to Sukkah *5.5, "They blew never less than twenty-one blasts in the Temple (in a day) and never more than forty-eight." So, on days that were not Sabbath or Feast days, the priests blew seven times, each time three blasts as the preceding verse explains "a sustained, a quavering and another sustained blast" (*T'kiah, T'ruah *and* T'kiah*). The first three blasts were made when the gates of the Temple were opened, nine during the morning sacrifice and nine at the evening sacrifice. The Sabbath was also announced with three blasts of the trumpet and again three more blasts were made when the Sabbath had actually begun.*

Music in the Temple

The music of the Temple was as splendid as its wealth. It included both vocal and instrumental music with, as Edersheim puts it, the real service of praise in the Temple being only with the voice. Instrumental music was for accompaniment only. The vocal music consisted of extracts from the Psalms and other poetic sections from Scripture. The Mishnaic tractate *Tamid* (The Daily Whole-Offering) lists the psalms that were sung on the various week-days when the drink-offering was poured out.

There was a special psalm, Psalm 92, with the title "A Psalm: a song for the Sabbath Day." Feast-days had their own designated psalms. During the rejoicing of the *Beit ha-Sho'eva* festival (Festival of Water-drawing), the fifteen Psalms of Ascents (Psalms 120–134) were sung. The *Hallel*, which consisted of Psalms 113–118, was sung on feast-days during the sacrifices of the people.

Only the Levites were allowed to sing and there was a special Platform (*Duchan*) for them to stand on, between the Court of the Israelites and the Court of the Priests (*Middot* 2.6) while singing the daily Psalm. The Levitical choir stood on the fifteen semi-circular steps leading up to the Nicanor Gate when singing on special occasions.

Ordinary priests and Israelites of impeccable lineage were allowed to play instrumental music. Instrumental music to accompany Scriptural words dates back to King David. As Edersheim puts it, "The music of the Temple owed its origin to David, who was not only a poet and a musical composer, but who also invented musical instruments (Amos 6.5), especially the ten stringed *Nevel* or Lute" (p. 54). The Mishnah records (*Arakhin* 2.3) that "they played on never less than two harps or more than six, and on never less than two flutes."

The Rabbis mention thirty-six different instruments but the most important instrument in the Temple service was the trumpet. The occasions when the trumpet was used is listed in *Sukkah* 5.5.

The Priestly Functions

In his evocation of the Temple, Edersheim next passes on to the priesthood, laying the foundation for the subject with a description of the Levitical priesthood. He brings the focus to the period in hand, however, stating that "our present task rather is to trace its further development to what it was at the time when Jesus was in the Temple" (p. 62).

Edersheim points out that "In all these respects there was a difference between Israel and the tribe of Levi; between the family of Aaron; and finally, between an ordinary priest and the high-priest, who most fully typified our Great High-Priest, in whom all these symbols found their reality" (p. 86). The chart here tabulates the priests in order of rank. The High Priest held the supreme position as the one who alone held the privilege of performing ritual of the deepest religious significance. Next in line was the Captain of the Temple or *Segan*, who is sometimes described as a kind of deputy High Priest whose function was to act as a substitute when the High Priest could not be present. However, it is clear from both Josephus (*War* 6.294) and the New Testament (Acts 4.1) that his position entitled him also to supervise all the arrangements for keeping order in the area of the Temple.

Also among the chief priests but below the Captain of the Temple were the twenty-four leaders of the weekly courses of priests (*Rosh ha-Mishmar*) and then the directors of the daily courses (*Rosh Beit Ab*). The arrangement of the priesthood into 24 courses apparently dates from the time of David and Solomon up to the Babylonian captivity. Edersheim records a little-known fact which gives a fascinating background to the scene of the appearance of the angel to Zechariah as he was burning incense.

He writes, "Only four out of the twenty-four 'courses' returned: those of Jedaiah, Immer, Pashur, and Harim, the course of 'Jedaiah' being placed first because it was of the high-priest's family, 'of the house of Jeshua, the son of Jozadak.' To restore the original number, each of these four families was directed to draw five lots for those which had not returned, so as to form once more twenty-four courses, which were to bear the ancient names. Thus, for example, Zacharias, the father of John the Baptist, did not really belong to the family of Abijah, which had not returned from Babylon, but to the 'course of Abia,' which had been formed out of some other family, and only bore the ancient name" (p. 87). Apart from the three pilgrim festivals, these men were obliged to come to the Temple twice a year (one week out of twenty-four).

The Temple overseers (*Amarkelim*) were also counted among the chief priests. It would appear from the sources that they held the keys of the Temple and a certain power of supervision, but under the Captain of the Temple. There could be no less than seven *Amarkelim*. The Treasurers (*Gizbarim*), also never less than seven, looked after all the financial affairs of the Temple.

The ordinary priests (*Cohanim*) were lower in hierarchy to all those already mentioned. The Levites, lower still, acted as assistants to the priests in their work.

THE PRIESTLY FUNCTIONS

1. THE HIGH PRIEST
(ha-Cohen ha-Gadol)

2. THE CHIEF PRIESTS:

Captain of the Temple
(Segan)

Leaders of the 24 Weekly Courses
(Rosh ha-Mishmar)
& their Daily Courses
(Rosh Beit Ab)

Temple Overseers
(Amarkelim)

Temple Treasurers
(Gizbarim)

3. THE PRIESTS
(Cohanim)

4. THE LEVITES
(Leviim)

Chart of the priestly functions in order of rank.

The High Priest

As Edersheim writes, "the whole characteristics and the functions of the priesthood centred in the person of the high-priest" (p. 61). His unique position meant that special purity and holiness were expected of him. He had to be totally free of all physical defects and stringent rules applied as to whom he was allowed to marry. Leviticus 21.13–15 stipulates that he had to marry a virgin. He was forbidden to take a widow, divorcee, a woman who had been violated, or a prostitute. In rabbinical times, the concept of a virgin was narrowed down to girls between twelve and twelve-and-a-half years of age (Mishnah, *Yebamoth* 6.4).

In practice, many of the High Priests married daughters of priests. A well-known example from the New Testament is of the High Priest Caiaphas who married the daughter of the High Priest Annas (John 18.13). According to biblical tradition, the High Priest came from a Zadokite high-priestly aristocracy, with the office held for life and hereditary. The anointing of the High Priest, as prescribed in Exodus 29, had ceased as a practice. In the Second Temple period, the office was passed on by investiture with the high-priestly garments, and was subject to nepotism, much bribery and corruption.

The death of the High Priest had the power of atonement. On his death, all those guilty of taking a life and who had fled to one of the "cities of refuge" appointed in Numbers 35, could return to their homes. A fascinating insight into the practical workings of this law is illustrated in the Mishnaic tractate, *Makkoth* 2.6, where we learn that the mothers of High Priests used to send food and clothing to these homicides to deter them from praying for the death of their sons!

*The breastplate, which was worn over the ephod, was composed of twelve precious stones, each representing one of the tribes of Israel. The original "*Urim *and* Thummim*" (Lights and Perfections), which was used to ascertain the divine will, had been lost and replaced with the breastplate used by the priests during the Second Temple period.*

The most important function of the High Priest was, of course, his service on *Yom Kippur*—the Day of Atonement. In addition he usually participated in the burning of the Red Heifer. Josephus relates (*Antiquities* 15.408) that he frequently participated in the services of the Sabbath and Feast days as well. The High Priest also functioned as head of the Sanhedrin.

The High Priest was elaborately attired—first in the priestly vestments, the white linen robe, the white linen trousers, the turban and the girdle. Over these went four special items: the breastplate, the ephod, the tunic, and the golden frontlet which attached to the turban. The tunic was a rich dark blue color and from its hem hung pomegranates of blue, purple and scarlet alternating with golden bells. Over this went the ephod, which was a kind of apron with shoulder straps, made of white, blue, purple and scarlet, and embroidered with gold threads. Over this went the breastplate.

*The gold frontlet (*ziz*) symbolized the holiness that the High Priest was supposed to manifest to God; it bore the words "Holiness to* Yahweh.*"*

(overleaf) A priest at work on the Golden Vine.

The Tasks of the Priests

It is estimated that the priests on duty for the daily public sacrifices numbered at least fifty. A weekly course consisted of, on average, six daily courses, and so we have about three hundred priests for each weekly course.

Two extracts from the Mishnah confirm this. The first extract states that when the veil of the Temple needed to be washed, three hundred priests immersed it (*Shekalim* 8.5). The second is again in *Middot* 3.8, where it is written that when a leaf or a berry or a cluster was given as a freewill-offering to be hung on the Golden Vine, the offerer gave it to the priests to hang on this great symbolic representation of the nation. The Mishnah notes that Rabbi Eliezer ben Zadok, who lived in Jerusalem prior to the destruction of the Temple, said, "It once happened that three hundred priests were appointed thereto." Next to the priest's ladder in this illustration of the Golden Vine, one of the golden chains which hung from the roof of the Porch can be seen. These allowed the priests to climb up to see the crown-shaped pediments of the Porch windows.

If there were approximately three hundred priests on duty for each weekly course and you multiply this by twenty-four, the number of courses, this comes to seven thousand and two hundred priests!

The Levites were also divided into courses of service. The ranks of the Levites were greatly reduced after the return from Babylon; the records in Ezra and Nehemiah indicate that less than four hundred Levites returned. Their numbers were supplemented by the Nethinim, "given ones" who were probably non-Israelite in origin. The total number of Levites at the time of Christ has been estimated at nine thousand and six hundred.

Edersheim offers an interesting insight into the priesthood, writing that "Among the most interesting glimpses of early life in the church is that afforded by a small piece of rapidly-drawn scenery which presents to our view 'a great company of the priests,' obedient to the faith. We seem to be carried back in imagination to the time when Levi remained faithful amidst the general spiritual defection, and then through the long vista of devout ministering priests to reach the fulfilment of this saying of Malachi—part admonition, and part prophecy: 'For the priest's lips should keep knowledge, and they should seek the law at his mouth: for he is the messenger of the Lord of hosts.' We can picture to ourselves how they who ministered in holy things would at eventide, when the Temple was deserted of its worshippers, gather to speak of the spiritual meaning of the services, and to consider the wonderful things which had taken place in Jerusalem, as some alleged, in fulfilment of those very types that formed the essence of their office and ministry. 'For this thing was not done in a corner.'" (p. 58,59).

The entire priesthood was descended from the family of Levi, one of Jacob's twelve sons. The Levites had no distinction other than belonging to this particular tribe of Israel who had stood up for the truth in the time of Moses. The priests were descended from Aaron, a notable Levite, while the High Priest was supposed to trace his genealogy back to Zadok, a notable of the family of Aaron.

Levites, like ordinary Israelites, were forbidden, on pain of death, from entering the Sanctuary, so that all the tasks which involved the maintenance of the Temple proper were the priests' responsibility. The Levites' tasks were restricted to providing the singing and instrumental music for the Temple ritual and to carry out lesser tasks than those undertaken by the priests. They were in charge of opening and closing the outer doors of the Temple complex while the priests had the charge of the inner doors. They also provided the police force of the Temple area.

*Priests wearing their white garments and working in the cells that surrounded the Temple. Both Josephus (*War *5.220–221) and* Middot *4.3 record there being cells arranged in three storeys round the Sanctuary and the Holy of Holies. These 38 cells rested on cubit wide ledges on the sides of the Sanctuary, like the chambers or* yatsiot *of Solomon's Temple (1 Kings 6.5). They appear to have been used to store vessels and materials for the Temple ritual and the ongoing nature of this ritual meant that their maintenance must have entailed much labor.*

The Sacrificial Offerings

As Edersheim writes, "so complicated a service and one which enjoined such frequent sacrifices, must always have kept a large number of priests busy in the courts of the Temple" (p. 111). The sacrifices offered in the Second Temple were essentially the same as those laid down in the Law or Torah. Man was understood to be in a state of defilement, in constant need of cleansing in all the aspects of his life, from his birth up to his death. The institution of sacrifice in the Law of Moses enjoined that "the life of the flesh is in the blood" (Lev. 17.11) and that "it is the blood that maketh atonement for the soul."

Edersheim writes that the sacrifices of the Old Testament were symbolical and typical—they necessarily pointed to a mediatorial priesthood and finally to "He whose priesthood was perfect and who on a perfect altar brought a perfect sacrifice, once for all—a perfect Substitute (more correctly rendered 'representative'—L.R.) and a perfect Mediator" (p. 82).

Apart from the animals offered as burnt, sin, trespass or peace offerings, meat-offerings (which ought to be translated "meal-offerings") were also used as sacrifices. These were either public, like the twelve loaves of shewbread renewed every Sabbath day, or private, such as the daily meal-offering of the High Priest or in substitution for a sin-offering if the offerer could not afford a more expensive animal. An offering of wine, which indicated love, always accompanied the meal-offering.

Particular sacrifices that were offered on the various festivals all fell under one of the four main offerings shown on the chart. Some have suggested that the first three offerings were for different degrees of sin. The burnt offering, for when there was no particular

Edersheim records that three kinds of four-footed beasts—oxen, sheep and goats—and two kinds of birds—turtle-doves and young pigeons—were used for sacrifice. Leviticus stipulates that the offering to the Lord was to be "of the cattle, of the herd and of the flock." The oxen represented strength, the sheep innocent submission and the goat, an assertive animal, the mind of the flesh. Turtle-doves or young pigeons were fitting types of the harmlessness of the Son of God "holy, harmless, undefiled."

MAIN OFFERINGS

BURNT *(OLAH)*:
The entire surrender to God of an individual or the congregation

SIN *(CHATAT)*:
To make atonement for the person of the offender—to cover our sinful nature

TRESPASS *(ASHAM)*:
To make atonement for a specific offence done in ignorance

PEACE *(SHELAMIM)*:
To complete other sacrifices which always preceded it

offense, was used to atone for the unclean state of human nature. This is typical of the sacrifice of Christ. It was offered as a regular morning and evening sacrifice and was always a male animal. The blood was thrown on the angle of the Altar below the red line.

With regard to the sin offering, public offerings of this kind were always male animals, while private offerings were female. The blood of such sacrifices was sprinkled on the four horns of the Altar.

As the name implies, the trespass offering was made in cases of disobedience to a specific law. Leviticus 5 enumerates examples such as the contracting of defilement, violence or the making of an unlawful oath. In these cases, the blood of the sacrifice was sprinkled on the corners of the Altar, below the red line.

Finally, the peace offerings also had to be a living creature for sacrifice, but offered out of pure love at the completion of other sacrifices. This could be a female animal, being a subordinate sacrifice, in order to show that the woman had a part in redemption through womankind's bearing of Messiah through Mary (1 Tim. 2.15). Its blood was always sprinkled on the four horns of the Altar.

In his chapter called "At night in the Temple," Edersheim suggests that the apostle John had been a priest because of the frequent analogies to the Temple ritual contained in the Gospel written by him and also in the Book of Revelation. Only someone who had taken an active part in the Temple service could use the imagery of the Temple in such a natural way.

Edersheim gives an example from the Book of Revelation. First, he sets the scene of nighttime in the Temple, describing the changing of the priests who had fulfilled their duty for the day with those who were coming up from their quarters in the Ophel to prepare for the service the following day. It was the duty of the Levites to guard the gates of the Temple Mount to prevent anyone unclean from entering. The Levites guarded twenty-four stations. Edersheim estimates that 240 Levites and thirty priests were on duty on any one night. The night was divided into watches, with the last watch before dawn considered the most difficult in which to stay awake. Edersheim suggests that the admonition to the believers in Revelation 16.15—"Blessed is he that watcheth and keepeth his garments, lest he walk naked and they see his shame"—derived from John's own experience of guard duty in the Temple.

Some priests slept in the Chamber of the Hearth, where a fire was kept burning continually. If they suffered ritual uncleanliness, they could go down to the Chamber of Immersion (*Beit ha-T'vilah*) to bathe and regain a state of purity. According to *Tamid* 1.2, the officer came to call the priests at varying times: "Sometimes he came at cockcrow and sometimes a little sooner or later," which again brings to mind

(overleaf) At night in the Temple, showing the torch-bearing priests preparing for the service of the following day.

the words of Jesus. "Watch ye therefore: for ye know not when the master of the house cometh, at even, or at midnight, or at the cockcrowing, or in the morning: Lest coming suddenly he find you sleeping. And what I say unto you I say unto all, Watch" (Mark 13.35–37).

The priests in the Chamber of the Hearth then gave the keys of the Temple Court to the officer in charge of the lots who, according to the tractate *Shekalim* (5.1), was one Mattityahu ben Samuel. He then entered the Temple Court with two groups of torch-bearing priests, who separated and completed a circuit of the Temple colonnades, checking that all was ready for the day's service before the opening of the Nicanor Gate. The priests then went to the Chamber of Hewn Stone, where the lots were cast to decide the priests' duties for the day.

The Priestly Lots

Lots were cast to decide which priests would perform the various tasks necessitated by the Temple service on a daily basis. The first lot was cast earlier as it decided who was to clear the Altar (*ha-Mizbe'ach*) and prepare it for the day's sacrifices. The first sound to be heard was that of the Laver (*ha-Kior*), in which the priest whose task it was to clear the Altar washed. He then took a silver firepan and ascended the ramp to the Altar and cleared away the cinders that remained. On his descent, his assistants also washed and mounted the Altar with shovels and rakes, to move aside the remains of the previous day's sacrifice. All the ashes were raked onto the center of the Altar and were removed once a large pile had accumulated. The designated priest then prepared two fires (*Tamid* 2.5), apart from the fire that was kept burning continually on the Altar. One fire was used to produce coals for the Incense Altar that stood within the Holy Place. The other fire was used for the daily sacrifices.

THE LOTS OF THE PRIESTS

LOT 1. Cleaning the Altar and preparing it for the day's sacrifices	**LOT 3.** Offering up the incense
LOT 2. Killing the sacrificial animal, cleaning the Lampstand and the Altar of Incense	**LOT 4.** Laying the pieces of the sacrificial animal on the Altar and concluding the sacrifice

Then all the priests repaired to the Chamber of Hewn Stone (*Lishkat ha-Gazit*), where the next three lots would be cast to decide who would perform the other tasks involved in the day's service. The second lot decided who would kill the sacrificial animal and clean the Lampstand and the Incense Altar. Before the lamb for the morning sacrifice could be slaughtered, the officer in charge of the lots would ask, "Is the sky lit up as far as Hebron?" Once this condition was met, a lamb was brought from the Chamber of the Lambs and slaughtered in the Shambles at the same time that the door to the Sanctuary was opened. The blood of the sacrificial animal was caught in a golden bowl and sprinkled on the Altar. The remainder of the blood was poured onto the base of the Altar. Pieces of the animal were placed on the ramp ready for the priest who was chosen for the fourth lot, to lay on the Altar of Sacrifice.

The most coveted lot was the third, which decided who would burn the incense. Rarely was this privilege granted more than once in a lifetime. As mentioned, the fourth lot decided who would lay the pieces of the sacrifice, which was already prepared, on the Altar. It also included the offering of both the meal and drink offerings to conclude the sacrifice.

*The brass Laver, situated between the Temple Porch and the Altar. The Mishnah cites a special wooden device on the Laver made by a person called Ben Katin (*Yoma *3.10,* Tamid *1.4, 3.8). This device could be heard as far as Jericho, its sound signalling the start of the day's service in the Temple.*

The Laver

Before the priest on whom the lot had fallen to clean the Altar and start up its fires could proceed with his duties, he had first to wash in the Laver. *Tamid* 1.4 records that the other priests admonished him: "Take heed that thou touch not the vessel before thou hast sanctified thy hands and feet in the laver."

Edersheim describes the method of washing. He writes that "hands and feet were washed by laying the right hand on the right foot and the left hand on the left" (p. 130) and raises the question that this might have been what Jesus referred to in John 13.10: "He that is washed needeth not save to wash his feet, but is clean every whit." This is another of the instances that would confirm Edersheim in his belief that John had originally been a Temple priest.

The Shambles, or Place of Slaughter, where the sacrificial animals were slain. It is located in the Court of the Priests, just to the north of the Altar.

The Shambles

As soon as Mattityahu ben Samuel had received confirmation that the sky was bright as far as Hebron, he said, "Go and bring a lamb from the Chamber of the Lambs." The lambs were kept in the northwest corner of the Temple. The lamb that had already been inspected the night before was again inspected by the light of torches and given water from a golden bowl. He who had drawn the second lot then dragged the lamb to the Shambles (*Beit ha-Mitbachim*).

The Place of Slaughter consisted of twenty-four rings arranged in rows into which the heads of the sacrificial animals were placed. The Shambles proper were eight short pillars on which rested blocks of cedar with hooks for hanging the slaughtered animals. The marble tables between the pillars were used to slay the sacrifices. The method of slaying the animal was carefully stipulated. Firstly, the animal was killed only after the great gate which led into the Sanctuary itself was opened. Having heard the gate open, the designated priest tied the animal to the second ring in the northwestern corner of the Place of Slaughter. Its legs were bound together and its head was put through the ring facing west. The sacrificial animal was slaughtered with a knife and its blood caught in a golden bowl to be sprinkled on the Altar.

The blood of the lamb for the morning sacrifice was collected in the golden bowl and sprinkled in the stipulated manner on the Altar. This had to be done in the form of the Greek letter *Gamma* (γ) on two sides below the red line. The remainder of the blood was poured out at the base of the Altar.

The original Altar of Burnt Sacrifice built in the Wilderness of Sinai was made of shittim wood overlaid with brass. It measured 5 cubits (8.6 ft., 2.63 m) long by 5 cubits wide and was 3 cubits (5.2 ft., 1.58 m) high. It had horns at the four corners and four rings in which to insert staves to carry it when moving the camp of Israel from one place to another.

The Altar in the Second Temple was also four-square but, as it did not need to be portable, was made of untooled stones as stipulated in Exodus 20.25: "and if thou wilt make me an altar of stone, thou shalt not build it of hewn stone: for if thou lift up thy tool upon it thou hast polluted it."

There is no mention of a red line on the Altar of the Tabernacle in the Wilderness or on that in the Temple of Solomon. The Rabbis placed great store on the later laws which stipulated where the blood was to be sprinkled, with clear instructions as to when the blood should be sprinkled above or below the red line. If this was done improperly, the sacrifice became invalid. *Middot* (3.2) also describes the outlet of "two holes like two narrow nostrils" at the base of the Altar where the remainder of the blood was sometimes poured, to go down a water channel into the Kedron Valley.

The ramp of the Altar was made of untooled stones taken from the nearby valley of Beth-haccherem. They were whitened to remove the blood stains at the Feast of Passover and at the Feast of Tabernacles.

The Altar of Burnt Sacrifice. Its measurements are open to dispute because of discrepancies between Josephus and the Mishnah. Middot *3.1 describes it as being four-square, originally 32 cubits by 32 cubits, but records changes in size following the Exile. It does not give its height. Josephus gives the dimensions as 50 cubits by 50 cubits with a height of 15 cubits (these measurements are, however, too large). A ledge for the priests to walk around the Altar while they tended the sacrifices was known as the "circuit."*

The ramp of the Altar is based on the stipulation in Exodus (20.26): "neither shalt thou go up by steps unto mine altar, that thy nakedness be not discovered thereon."

The Lampstand

Returning to the lots which decided who would perform the service for the day, we find that the second lot, which determined who would slay the sacrifice, also decided who would clean the Lampstand and the Altar of Incense.

The priest on whom the lot had fallen tends the golden Lampstand in the Holy Place. He had waited as close as possible to the time that the blood of the morning sacrifice was sprinkled on the Altar of Burnt Offering. *Tamid* 3.9 describes the stone with three steps cut into it in front of the Lampstand. The priest stood on this stone to trim the lamps. It is recorded that if the two easternmost lamps were burning, the priest would trim the other lamps but leave these two burning. If these had gone out, he trimmed them and lit them from others that were still alight and then trimmed the rest.

As to the form of the Lampstand or Menorah, Edersheim writes that its form is known from its representation on the Arch of Titus in Rome. Here, it is depicted as a seven-branched lampstand standing on a solid hexagonal base on which were depictions of two eagles holding a wreath and dragons with heads of birds and wings. This form of the Menorah was chosen as the national symbol of the State of Israel in 1949. However, even then there was criticism that the base was actually derived from pagan symbolism. Archaeological finds such as the menorah found engraved on the walls of one of the Herodian villas excavated in the Jewish Quarter in Jerusalem indicate that the original Menorah of the Second Temple actually had a tripod base. It is now believed that it was during the reign of Herod the Great, who tried to reconcile Roman ways with Jewish sensibilities, that the base of the Menorah was changed to one that might be admired by his Roman overlords. In any case, it was not the original Lampstand that had been built in the wilderness journey; that lampstand must have been lost before the Temple of Solomon was built, when it was recorded that there were ten golden lampstands in the Holy Place (1 Kings 7.49).

The lampstand depicted on the Arch of Titus in Rome.

The Incense Altar

The priest cast in the third lot performed the incense offering in the Holy Place. Earlier, one of the priests of the second lot would have waited until the lamb was being slain before clearing the Incense Altar of ashes. The tractate *Tamid* records the elaborate procedure from the clearing of the ashes to the actual task of offering incense. The priest of the second lot cleared the ashes into an ash-bin with both hands and left it in the Sanctuary. After the sacrifice, he returned to take the ash-bin after having prostrated himself in the Holy Place.

Meanwhile, coals for burning the incense had been prepared on the Great Altar. Fine pieces of fig-tree wood piled near the southwest were used for this fire. A priest went up to the Altar, scooped the burning coals from the fire into a silver firepan and then came down and emptied it into the golden firepan reserved for this purpose. He then took this firepan into the Holy Place and piled the coals on the Incense Altar, smoothed them down with the back of the firepan and came out, after prostrating himself.

We know the form of the Incense Altar from its description in Exodus 30.1–10. It was made of shittim wood, overlaid with gold. Its top was square in shape and measured 1 cubit by 1 cubit (1.72 ft., 0.53 m). It stood 2 cubits high (3.44 ft., 1.05 m) and had horns on each of the four corners. A crown of gold surrounded the top part of the Altar. Originally, the incense was com-

(opposite page) A priest tending the Lampstand in the Holy Place.

A priest offering incense.

posed of the four ingredients stipulated in Exodus 30.34–36: stacte, onycha, galbanum and frankincense. However, by the time of the Second Temple, rabbinic traditions had added other components. Josephus, in his *Jewish War* (5.218) mentions that "thirteen fragrant spices" were used on the Incense Altar: myrrh, cassia, spikenard, saffron, costus, mace, cinnamon, salt and a herb which when added to the other components caused the smoke to rise in a straight column.

Shekalim 5.1 records that the Abtinas family was responsible for producing the incense, while *Yoma* 3.11 adds that they refused to share their knowledge with anyone outside the family. It is thought that the priestly family of Bar Kathros may have assisted or succeeded the Abtinas family. During the Jewish Quarter excavations, a home belonging to Bar Kathros was found with archaeological evidence that spices were mixed there.

The task of offering the incense was thought to confer a blessing on the offerer. The two remaining wicks on the Lampstand were lit just before the incense was blessed. The offerer had two assistants who withdrew, leaving the offerer alone in the Sanctuary.

As he crossed the courtyard with his helpers, a priest made a sound with the *Magrephah*, which apparently was a type of gong and a signal for the Levites to convene for the singing of Psalms and for those in a state of impurity to assemble at the Eastern Gate. The incense offerer awaited a signal from the presiding priest and then carefully laid the incense on the burning coals.

Incense was again offered in the evening at the ninth hour—the "hour of prayer"—by a priest chosen by the casting of an additional lot. This was the background to the healing of the lame man by Peter and John in Acts 3. It was also most probably the time that Zechariah, while offering incense, had an angelic visitation that told him that he was to become the father of John the Baptist, the forerunner of the Messiah (Luke 1.9–22).

The Blessing of the Priests

Traditional prayers were offered at the time of incense. With the offering of prayers completed, the priests who had performed their appointed tasks came and stood on the steps of the porch carrying the implements they had used to perform their various duties. As recorded in *Tamid* 7.2, "one had the ash-bin, another the oil-jug, another the firepan, another the incense dish, another the ladle and its cover."

In the meantime, the priest on whom had fallen the fourth lot, to place the sacrifice on the Altar, ascended the ramp of the Altar, where his assistants passed him the pieces of the sacrificial animal. He laid his hand on each of the pieces and flung them into the fire on the Altar. The priests who were waiting on the steps then raised their hands above their heads and pronounced the priestly blessing of Numbers 6.24–26:

"The Lord bless thee and keep thee: the Lord make His face shine upon thee, and be gracious unto thee: the Lord lift up his countenance upon thee, and give thee peace." *Tamid* 7.2 records that in the Temple they pronounced the name when reciting the blessing, while in the provinces another name was substituted.

In an interesting aside, Edersheim points out that "if it had been the duty of Zecharias as incensing priest for the day, to lead in the priestly blessing, we can all the better understand the wonder of the people as 'he beckoned unto them, and remained speechless,' while they waited for his benediction" (p. 142). The Blessing of the Priests was generally given at this stage of the evening sacrifice and is not generally associated with the morning sacrifice.

Reciting the Priestly Blessing (Num. 6.24–26) at the entrance to the Sanctuary.

The Levitical Choir

(opposite) The Levitical choir on the fifteen semi-circular steps, in front of the Nicanor Gate.

After the priestly blessing, the task of the priest of the fourth lot was to perform the meal-offering and the drink-offering or libation. Two silver trumpets were blown, the drink-offering was passed around the base of the Altar and Ben Arza, who we learn from *Shekalim* 5.1 was officer over the cymbals, clashed his instrument as a signal for the Levites to begin singing.

The Levites stood on the fifteen semi-circular steps between the Court of the Women and the Court of Israel in the Nicanor Gate. These steps were shaped, as lyrically described in the Mishnah, like one half of a round threshing floor (*Middot* 2.5). The Levitical choir, accompanied by musicians, sang the Psalm appointed for that day. According to *Tamid* 7.4, Psalms 24, 48, 82, 94, 81 and 93 were sung in order on weekdays, while Psalm 92 ("A Psalm, song for the sabbath day") was sung on the Sabbath. The choir included some sons of the Levites whose young voices must have added an extra dimension to this part of the Temple ritual—the Levites were never allowed in the Court of the Priests, for this court was reserved for priests alone. The psalm for the day was always sung in sections. Thus, when a break in the singing occurred, the priests blew their trumpets and the people prostrated themselves. The singing of the daily psalm marked the end of the morning service.

The rest of the day, up to the time of the evening sacrifice at the ninth hour (between 2 and 3 p.m.), was taken up with sacrifices and offerings brought by the Israelites. The evening sacrifice followed the same procedure as that of the morning, apart from the fact that lots were cast only to determine who would offer the incense (the other lots remained the same). Also, the incense was burned after, not before the pieces of sacrifice were laid on the Altar.

Sabbath in the Temple

On the Sabbath, of course, not only was the special psalm for the Sabbath day sung, but there were other changes in the Temple ritual as well. The main ritual of the Sanctuary associated with the Sabbath in Scripture was the changing of the shewbread on the Table of Shewbread (Lev. 24.5–9). Leviticus 23.3 stipulates also that there should be "a holy convocation" or assembly and Numbers 28.9–10 that two lambs along with the meal and drink offerings be offered as a special Sabbath offering.

Edersheim points out that the Sabbath was not just a weekly festival or a memorial of the original hallowing of the seventh day when God rested from His work of creation. The fourth of the Ten Commandments given by Moses enjoins Israelites to observe the Sabbath day because of their deliverance from Egypt and to "remember that thou wast a servant in the land of Egypt and that the Lord thy God brought thee out thence through a mighty hand and by a stretched out arm: Therefore the LORD thy God commanded thee to keep the sabbath day" (Deut. 5.15). He also quotes Hebrews 4.9, "There remaineth therefore a rest (Greek—keeping of a sabbath) to the people of God," which indicates that its great purpose was to point forward to what he calls "the eternal Sabbath of completed work, of completed redemption and completed hallowing" (p. 146).

The Table of Shewbread in the Sanctuary.

By the time of Christ, this weekly feast of the Sabbath was weighted down by rabbinical injunctions. The Mishnah has a tractate solely devoted to the laws concerning its observance. This tractate, called *Shabbath*, details the decrees of both the School of Shammai and the School of Hillel which varied in their strictures. It was against a background of such stringent rules that Christ healed on the Sabbath (Luke 13.10–17) and plucked off the ears of corn, invoking the wrath of the Jewish rulers and Pharisees (Mark 2.23–28).

The Table of Shewbread stood in the Holy Place oriented east-west. It was made of shittim wood, overlaid with gold and measured 2 cubits (3.44 ft., 1.05 m) long by 1 cubit (20.67 inches, 0.53 m) wide and stood 1.5 cubits (2.58 ft., 0.79 m) high. It had a gold crown of wreathen work around the top of it. Two rows or piles of unleavened bread were placed on the table. These were called the shewbread, but the Hebrew literally means "bread of faces." This is understood to mean that each bread represented one of the tribes of Israel with their "faces" lifted up toward God. Because of the reference to dishes and covers, etc., in the description of the Table of Shewbread in Exodus 25.29, some illustrations show an elaborate structure with a separate tier, supported by frames, for each bread, rising from the table. This is, however, a rabbinic interpretation. A bowl of frankincense was placed on top of each pile of bread, "for a memorial" (Lev. 24.7). The shewbread of the previous week was exchanged on the Sabbath for freshly baked bread. This service was performed by the new course of priests for the succeeding week. Jesus referred to the eating of the old shewbread by the priests on one of the occasions when he opposed strict sabbatarianism, saying in Matthew 12.5–8, "Have ye not read in the Law how that on the sabbath days the priests in the Temple profane the sabbath and are blameless? but I say unto you that in this place is one greater than the temple ...for the Son of man is Lord even of the sabbath day."

In his section on the Sabbath, Edersheim makes a small but fascinating digression on the observance of the Sabbatical Year in the time of Christ. The Sabbatical Year was part of the beautiful land law originally instituted by Moses, according to which, every seventh year, the land was not to be worked. "Six years thou shalt sow thy field, and in six years thou shalt prune thy vineyard and gather in the fruit thereof. But in the seventh year shall be a sabbath of rest unto the land, a sabbath for the LORD: thou shalt neither sow thy field nor prune thy vineyard" (Lev. 25.3–4).

Sadly, the observance of the sabbatical year was neglected for many years, as 2 Chronicles 36.21 explains that the seventy years' captivity in Babylon was to make restitution for 490 years during which it had not been kept. However, Edersheim points out that the observance of the Sabbatical Year was strictly enforced at the time of Christ.

Grapes on a vine in a Sabbatical Year. Whatever grew of itself in this year, for example grapes on the vine, as shown here, could be gathered by the poor to feed themselves. To enable the owners of the land to prepare for this seventh year of rest for the land, the wonderful provision was made whereby the land yielded a twofold increase which they could store for the seventh year.

The Jubilee Year, observed every fiftieth year, after a cycle of seven sabbatical years (Lev. 25.8–17), had, by this time, ceased to be kept.

Again the Mishnah has a tractate solely devoted to this aspect of the Law called *Shebiith* (or Seventh Year), which details the rabbinical injunctions concerning it. Here, also, there are differences in what was required by the School of Shammai and the School of Hillel. Apart from determining that the poor had an abundance of food available to them in this year, all debts were also remitted in the seventh year. As Edersheim points out, "Thus, as the Sabbath itself, so the Sabbatical year pointed forward to the 'rest which remaineth to the people of God,' when, contest and labour completed, they sing, 'on the other side of the flood,' the song of Moses and of the Lamb: 'Great and marvellous are thy works, Lord God Almighty; just and true are Thy ways, Thou King of saints. Who shall not fear Thee, O Lord, and glorify Thy name? for thou only art holy: for all nations shall come and worship before Thee; for thy judgments are made manifest'" (p. 164).

Calendar of Jewish Feasts

On the calendar that is unique to Israel Edersheim writes, "the symbolical character which is to be traced in all the institutions of the Old Testament appears also in the arrangement of its festive calendar" (p. 165). The number seven was the sacred unit of time measurement in Israel as opposed to those measurements used in the surrounding civilizations where time was divided by varying units of days. In the Egyptian civil calendar, for example, a month of thirty days was divided into three units of ten days each. The provision by the God of Israel of one day's rest in seven was divinely appointed both with the temporal welfare of man and his future hope in mind.

Apart from the Sabbath day, Edersheim shows just how much the number seven was impacted in the calendar of Israel: "Seven weeks after the commencement of the ecclesiastical year is the Feast of Pentecost: the seventh month is more sacred than the rest, its 'firstborn' or New Moon being not only devoted to the Lord like those of the other months, but specially celebrated as the 'Feast of Trumpets' while three other festivals occur within its course—the Day of Atonement, the Feast of Tabernacles, and its Octave. Similarly, each seventh year is Sabbatical and after seven times seven years comes that of the Jubilee" (p. 195). It was truly a calendar of supernatural design.

Three main feasts are stipulated in Exodus 23.14: "Three times thou shalt keep a feast unto me in the year." These refer to the three joyful festivals of Passover (*Pesach*), Weeks (*Shavuot*) and Tabernacles (*Succot*). They were also known as pilgrim festivals, as it was enjoined on all male Israelites to travel to Jerusalem for these festivals. They also corresponded with three main divisions of the agricultural year: Passover—Barley Harvest, Weeks—Wheat Harvest, and Tabernacles—the final Ingathering.

Apart from these Mosaic festivals, there were two additional feasts that were celebrated at the time of Christ: the Feast of the Dedication (Hanukkah), which was celebrated on the 25th of *Kislev*, and the Feast of Lots (Purim), celebrated on the 14th or 15th of *Adar*. The names of the months, as shown on the chart, were derived from those used in Babylonia. Most of the Hebrew names of the months have been lost apart from the four months mentioned in Scripture, whose meanings are linked with agricultural characteristics: *Abib*, the first month—sprouting or green ears, *Ziv*, the second month—splendor or flowering, *Ethanim*, the seventh month—flowing rivers, *Bul*, the eighth month—rain.

THE HEBREW CALENDAR

Sacred	Civil	Pre-Exilic	Post-Exilic	Feasts
1	7	Abib	Nisan	14 Passover (Pesach) Eve 15–21 Passover (Feast of Unleavened Bread) 16 Counting of the Omer begins (lasts 49 days, until Shavuot)
2	8	Ziv	Iyyar	
3	9		Sivan	6 Feast of Weeks or Pentecost (Shavuot)
4	10		Tammuz	
5	11		Ab	9 Destruction of the Temple
6	12		Elul	
7	1	Ethanim	Tishrei	1 New Year (Rosh Ha-Shanah) 10 Day of Atonement (Yom Kippur) 15–21 Feast of Tabernacles (Succot)
8	2	Bul	Heshvan	
9	3		Kislev	25 Dedication of the Temple (Hanukkah)
10	4		Tebet	
11	5		Shebat	
12	6		Adar	14,15 Purim
13			Ve-Adar	Intercalary month

The Feast of Passover

The feast of Passover (*Pesach*) took place during one of the months whose original biblical name *Abib* has come down to us. The Scripture records that it was to be to the Israelites their "beginning of months," which would commence the sacred year (the later name for this month was *Nisan*; *Tishrei*, the later name of the month *Ethanim*—mid-September to mid-October—began the civil year).

In a beautiful piece of writing, Edersheim points out that the three pilgrim feasts all had a threefold reference: firstly, to the time of year the feast took place; secondly, to an important event in the nation's history; and thirdly, as a type which pointed forward to a future fulfillment. Passover time occurred in Spring, the time when nature comes to life again after the stillness of winter (although strictly speaking the word *abib*, now used for Spring, actually refers not to a season but to a stage in the ripening of the barley). The countryside was in full bloom, the almond blossom a common sight on its hills and valleys.

In a historical sense, it was an annual celebration of deliverance from Egyptian bondage and the birth of Israel as a nation. That it was a type of things to come is made abundantly clear in the New Testament with Christ's frequent allusions to the Passover Meal and Paul's injunction to us: "Purge out therefore the old leaven that ye may be a new lump, as ye are unleavened. For even Christ our passover is sacrificed for us" (1 Cor. 5.7). It is also apparent in the Old Testament, from references such as the following, in Micah 7.15–16: "According to the days of thy coming out of the land of Egypt will I shew unto him marvellous things. The nations shall see and be confounded at all their might."

Passover time in the Land (a flowering almond tree).

The name *Pesach* means to "pass over" or "step over" and refers to how the Angel of Death passed over the houses of the Israelites as he slew the firstborn of the Egyptians (Exodus 12.27). As the first Passover was celebrated in Egypt prior to the Exodus of the Israelites, the way in which it was observed must have been different from how the feast would be commemorated henceforth. Originally, on the 10th of the month *Nisan*, the family head had to take an unblemished lamb or kid of the goats which was to be killed on the evening of the 14th, "between the evenings." The blood of the lamb or kid had to be sprinkled on the lintel and sideposts of each house and the animal had to be roasted and eaten with unleavened bread and bitter herbs. They were to eat the meal in haste ready for their journey.

The Mishnaic tractate *Pesachim* sup-

Jesus on the Temple terrace with the Rabbis. (Jesus is represented as the small figure in blue on the right of the terrace above the steps.)

plies details of how the Permanent Passover which lasted seven days as compared to the original one night was kept. Specific references to the keeping of this feast are made in the times of Kings Solomon and Hezekiah while King Josiah's Passover is a byword in history.

We have our first glimpse of Jesus during the Passover feast at the Temple in Jerusalem when he was twelve years old. Prior to this, Scripture is silent apart from the record of his birth. The account of Jesus' first visit to the Temple for the Passover feast is significant, as here his first words are recorded for us. Under the Law, attendance at the feasts in Jerusalem was obligatory for boys from the age of thirteen, when they would become a Son of the Commandment or *Bar Mitzvah*. In practice, this legal age was pushed forward by one or two years so that Jesus, after he had passed his twelfth year, came up to Jerusalem for the Passover with his family.

Multitudes of pilgrims would come from all parts of the country. The journey must have been joyous, with the Psalms of Ascents chanted by the pilgrims on their way up to Jerusalem. Jesus' first view of the Temple must have fortified in him the sense of the great purpose he had been developing during the quiet years in Nazareth. Attendance at the Temple was obligatory only for the first two days of Passover, after which many of the pilgrims returned home again. It would appear that Joseph and Mary did indeed begin to return home, but when they finally missed Jesus "it came to pass that after three days they found him in the temple, sitting in the midst of the doctors, both hearing them and asking them questions" (Luke 2.46).

It was the custom during the Passover for the Sanhedrin to come out on the Temple terrace or *Hel* and teach the people from the Scriptures. It was in the company of such scribes and teachers that Joseph and Mary found Jesus. It is tempting to speculate, in view of the typical nature of this feast, that Jesus posed questions concerning the sacrificial lamb and the great purpose which lay behind the solemnities of the Passover Feast.

The ritual of the Passover in the time of Christ began on the evening prior to the 14th of *Nisan*, when the head of each household supervised the search for any leaven in the home. A lamb that fulfilled the requirements of the original Passover sacrifice, "without blemish, a male of the first year" (Ex. 12.5), was purchased, usually from within the Temple precincts where the priests ran a thriving business in sacrificial animals. The lamb for the evening sacrifice was offered one hour earlier if the Passover fell on a weekday, and two hours earlier if it fell on the eve of a Sabbath. One Passover lamb was bought by each group of between twenty and thirty people (called a "company" in the Mishnah)—Edersheim points out that in the case of Jesus, his company consisted of himself and his disciples, with Peter and John responsible for the purchase and sacrifice of their communal lamb (Luke 22.8).

Next, the scene as enumerated in *Pesachim* 5.5–8 was enacted. Representatives of each company were divided into three groups of no less than thirty people each. The first group entered the Temple Court (or *Azarah*) with their Passover lambs and stood in the narrow Court of the Israelites while the Nicanor Gate was shut. Each individual slaughtered his own lamb while the event was announced by priests blowing on the silver trumpets. Next followed a ritual which differs completely from the Passover in Egypt. The priests stood in rows between the Court of the Israelites and the Altar, each alternate row holding silver bowls, the other gold. The first priest in each row caught the blood of one of the Passover lambs in a bowl, passed it on to the next priest, who, in turn, passed back an empty bowl to him so that there was a constant interchanging of blood-filled bowls for empty ones. The priests next to the Altar threw the sacrificial blood against the base of the Altar.

All the while this was going on, the Levites were singing the *Hallel* psalms (Ps. 113–118). Once the first group was finished, the remaining two groups came in by turn and slaughtered their lambs. The carcasses were then hung up, the stipulated pieces prepared for sacrifice and placed on the Great Altar. Only then could the incense offering be made and the lamps on the Lampstand trimmed (each offerer would roast his offering after nightfall). It only remained for the Temple Court to be washed by the priests from the copious blood shed during the Passover.

Passover in the Temple—a portrayal of the scene enumerated in tractate Pesachim *5.5–8.*

Modern-day Seder plate for Passover.

The present-day Jewish observance of the Passover differs greatly from that of the time of Christ, chiefly because of the absence of a Temple, which prevents the offering of sacrifices as prescribed in the Law of Moses. Thus, instead of a lamb, a roasted shankbone is placed on the right of the traditional *Seder* plate (which is the large dish used in the service celebrated in the home on the first night of Passover).

Arranged on the *Seder* plate are seven items deemed necessary for the keeping of the Passover. Going counterclockwise from the bone is a hard-boiled egg, representing the sacrifice offered on the 14th of *Nisan* in the Temple. Next is the *Haroset*, a mixture of apples, nuts, cinnamon and wine, which represents the mortar used by the Israelites to make bricks in Egypt. After that is a bowl of salt water, to remind the Jews of the tears shed in Egypt. A vegetable, usually parsley, is dipped in the salt water, apparently to maintain interest in the ceremony by any children that may be present. Finally, in the center of the dish is placed some bitter herbs, usually horseradish, which symbolizes the bitterness of bondage in Egypt. Three unleavened breads or *Matzot* are laid before the head of the house and four cups of wine are drunk, corresponding to the four expressions of redemption mentioned in Exodus 6.6–7. There is an extra cup of wine called the Cup of Elijah, and during the service the door is kept open to welcome the prophet whose return to the Jewish people is promised in Malachi 4.5–6.

The Passover service has clearly been formalized over the years but it still contains significant rites which preserve the typical nature of the feast. Edersheim, with his customary insight, points out that "we find in Rabbinic writings the 'Passover lamb' designated as 'His body'" and that "our special attention is called to the cup known as the 'cup of blessing' which we bless," and that "the very term for the Passover liturgy itself, the '*Haggadah*,' which means 'showing forth,' is exactly the same as that used by St. Paul in describing the service of the Lord's Supper" (pp. 198–199).

The Four Cups

Let us try to visualize the Passover Meal which Jesus turned into the Lord's Supper and left as an example of the memorial that believers in him were to keep every first day of the week. The feast took place in a large upper room in the city with simple furnishings arranged by Peter and John. From the Gospel record, we know that in the time of Christ, Israelites no longer partook of the feast in haste with their loins girded as they did when preparing to leave Egypt. Now that they were free, they dressed in their best clothes and ate the feast in a reclining position, as we read of John in his Gospel (13. 23) "Now there was leaning on Jesus' bosom one of his disciples, whom Jesus loved."

The table was prepared with the required items for the feast—the roast lamb, the unleavened bread, the bitter herbs and the *haroset* (similar to that used today). The four cups of wine stipulated in *Pesachim* 10.1 as obligatory to be drunk during the feast symbolize four expressions of redemption used in the words of God to Israel in Exodus 6.6–7:

"I will bring you out";
"I will rid you out of their bondage";
"I will redeem you";
"I will take you to me."

We can clearly trace reference to the drinking of these cups during the feast in the Gospel record. The feast began with the drinking of the first cup over which a benediction or giving of thanks was made. As Edersheim points out, "it was in all probability, in reference to the first cup that Luke gives the following account: 'And he took the cup and gave thanks and said, Take this and divide it among yourselves' (Luke 22.17)."

The procedure at the feast of Passover then stipulated that each participant wash his hands. Jesus used the opportunity to also wash his disciples' feet in order to impart to them a lesson on ministration. The Passover meal was then brought out. The head of the family or company dipped some of the bitter herbs in salt water, ate them and gave to the rest of the company. The various dishes were then temporarily removed and the second cup filled.

The four cups of wine drunk at Passover and at the Last Supper.

At this stage in the service, where children were present, the youngest child asks, "Why is this night different from all other nights?" The father responds by telling the story of the bondage and redemption of their people and the dishes were then returned to the table. The significance of the various items that comprised the Passover meal was expounded. The first part of the *Hallel* (Ps. 113–114) was then sung and the second cup drunk. Hands were washed again and one of the unleavened breads were broken with giving of thanks. Fragments of the bread were then sandwiched with bitter herbs and dipped in the *Haroset* and handed to each participant—the "sop" which Jesus gave to Judas before he went out to betray him would seem to correspond to this stage of the service.

Next came the eating of the supper itself. After the eating of the Passover Lamb, nothing more should have been eaten. However, as Edersheim explains "since the cessation of the Paschal sacrifice, the Jews conclude the supper with a piece of unleavened bread which they call the *Aphikomen*, or after-dish.

Now it is very remarkable that Our Lord seems so far to have anticipated the present Jewish practice that he break the bread 'when he had given thanks' instead of adhering to the old injunction of not eating anything after the Passover Lamb. And yet in so doing he only carried out the spirit of the Paschal feast, for as we have already explained, it was commemorative and typical. Hence, after the night of his betrayal, the Paschal lamb could have no further meaning and it was right that the commemorative *Aphikomen* should take its place" (p. 209).

Immediately following this, the third cup was drunk and thanks given for the meal. This would seem to equate with the "cup of blessing" (mentioned by Paul in 1 Cor. 10.16) as that associated with the institution of the Lord's Supper. Over the fourth cup, the singing of the *Hallel* was completed (Ps. 115–119). This corresponds with the reference in Mark's Gospel (14.26) which records that Jesus and his disciples "when they had sung an hymn (Greek-homnio-equivalent to the Hebrew *Hallel*), went out of the Mount of Olives."

Thus we find here in the *Aphikomen* the final piece of unleavened bread eaten at the end of the Passover Seder and in the third cup of the service, the original bread and wine used to institute the Lord's Supper which would commemorate "the Lord's death till he come" (1 Cor. 11.26).

The Feast of Weeks (Pentecost)

In Leviticus 23, the description of the Passover is immediately followed by the injunction "when ye be come into the land which I give you, and shall reap the harvest thereof, then ye shall bring a sheaf (Hebrew—*Omer*—a container holding about 5.1 pints) of the firstfruits of your harvest unto the priest" (v. 10). Now in the Land, the barley was just beginning to ripen—the name of the month *Abib*, which is another name for *Nisan*, takes its name from a word which meant "green ears of barley." Israelites were told that the priest "shall wave the sheaf (*Omer*) before the LORD, to be accepted for you: on the morrow after the sabbath the priest shall wave it" (Lev. 23.11).

A field of barley.

So, this waving of the *Omer* was included in the Feast of Unleavened Bread. Edersheim is of the opinion that "the morrow after the sabbath" referred to the day following the feast day of Passover, the 15th of *Nisan*. A more logical interpretation, however, appears to be the day after the weekly Sabbath. As part of the Feast of Unleavened Bread, it was also the beginning of the Feast of Firstfruits which would conclude fifty days later. Jesus is called "Christ the firstfruits" (1 Cor. 15.23) and with this waving of the sheaf, a lamb was also offered. "The morrow after the sabbath" was the very time, on the morning of the first day of the week, that Jesus rose from the dead. The waving of the *Omer* was an allusion to this great event. The

Feast of Unleavened Bread was a fitting preparation for the Feast of Firstfruits or *Shavuot*.

On a practical level, the priests selected the barley that was to be cut, "from a manured field or from an irrigated field or from a tree plantation" (*Menahoth* 8.2). The barley was sown seventy days before the Passover in a field that had been ploughed the previous year. To obtain one *Omer* of flour, ten full *Omers* of barley had to be cut down, thrashed, parched and ground into flour and then passed through a succession of sieves. The barley in the *Omer* was mixed with oil, a handful of frankincense was added and it was waved before God. A handful was taken and offered as a sacrifice on the altar. What was left over was eaten by the priests.

In Leviticus 23, after the stipulation of the waving of the *Omer*, we read, "and ye shall count unto you from the morrow after the sabbath, from the day that ye brought the sheaf (*Omer*) of the wave offering; seven sabbaths shall be complete: Even unto the morrow after the seventh sabbath shall ye number fifty days; and ye shall offer a new meat (meal) offering unto the LORD" (v. 15–16). So the waving of the *Omer* began the countdown to the next feast, the Feast of Weeks (*Shavuot*) or, as it is known in the New Testament, the Feast of Pentecost.

By this time, the harvest had ripened and summer had arrived. If Jesus' resurrection from the dead was the antitype of the waving of the *Omer* or firstfruits so, exactly seven weeks later, the outpouring of the Holy Spirit on the followers of Christ was the fulfillment of the second phase of firstfruits. Thus, the Feast of Unleavened Bread could almost be regarded as continuing until the end of the Feast of Weeks.

Two loaves of bread made of fine barley flour and leaven were brought to the priests as an offering to God. There was a special offering for the Feast of Weeks, as enumerated in Numbers 28.26–31: two young bullocks, one ram and seven year-old lambs. There were also festive offerings to accompany the waving of the two loaves. It is interesting to note that the Feast of Weeks is the only pilgrim feast to which no Mishnaic treatise is devoted. This festival must therefore have been regarded as of lesser importance than the others.

THE COUNTING OF THE OMER

Ye shall count unto you from the morrow after the sabbath, 7 sabbaths shall be complete.

ז	ו	ה	ד	ג	ב	א
יד	יג	יב	יא	י	ט	ח
כא	כ	יט	יח	יז	טז	טו
כח	כז	כו	כה	כד	כג	כב
לה	לד	לג	לב	לא	ל	כט
מב	מא	מ	לט	לח	לז	לו
מט	מח	מז	מו	מה	מד	מג

Chart, which is used today, showing the counting of the Omer. Each of the Hebrew letters has a numerical value, to count the fifty days from the Feast of Unleavened Bread to the Feast of Firstfruits.

The Feast of Tabernacles

The third of the great festivals, the Feast of Tabernacles (*Succot*), falls in the seventh month, the month of *Tishrei*. Edersheim writes of this month, in which the Day of Atonement (10th of *Tishrei*) also falls and which commences the civil year with the Feast of the Blowing of Trumpets, "What the seventh day, or Sabbath, was in reference to the week, the seventh month seems to have been in reference to the year. It closed not only the sacred cycle, but also the agricultural or working year. It also marked the change of seasons, the arrival of rain, of the winter equinox and determined alike the commencement and the close of the sabbatical year" (p. 235).

Tishrei is the time of year corresponding to September/October, when the days grow shorter and the clouds begin to gather in preparation for the early rain or *yoreh* that starts the rainy season. The activity in plant life is almost equal to the Spring, with the ripening of olives, dates, grapes, figs and pomegranates.

As mentioned, each of the major feasts has threefold significance. As regards to the season, the Feast of Tabernacles is the great feast of ingathering which takes place at a time when all the crops and fruits have been harvested, as commanded in Deuteronomy 16.13: "Thou shalt observe the feast of Tabernacles seven days, after that thou hast gathered in thy corn and thy wine." Its historical reference was to the dwelling of the Israelites in booths on their wilderness journey, while in type it pointed forward to the final harvest of life eternal in the Kingdom Age.

Pomegranates are a particularly noticeable feature of this season, their beautiful red fruits adorning trees throughout the country.

A modern-day succah *or booth, erected beside the Western Wall in Jerusalem during the Feast of Tabernacles. The requirements ascribed in the Mishnaic tractate* Sukkah *are observed to this day, although decorations have also been imported from other cultures in addition to the use of motifs from Judaism to adorn the interior.*

The Feast of Tabernacles begins on the 15th of *Tishrei* and continues until the 21st of the month, when it is followed by the Octave or Feast of the Eighth Day. The entire population had to obey the commandment "ye shall dwell in booths seven days, all that are Israelites born shall dwell in booths" (Lev. 23.42). It was a feast of great rejoicing, an annual encampment in the mellow days of Autumn, when the hard labor of harvest was over.

The types of trees used in making the booths were not specified; the four kinds of trees mentioned in Leviticus 23.40 probably refer to what the celebrants were to carry in their hands. In the time of Nehemiah, when they discovered that they had to keep the feast (Neh. 8.14), they used branches from the most common trees available such as olives, pines, myrtles and palms.

However, by the time the Mishnah had been compiled, the feast had been formalized and exact requirements for every element of its observance developed. The tractate *Sukkah* stipulates that the height of the booth not exceed 20 cubits nor be less than 10 handbreadths high and that three of its sides be closed in with branches.

While dwelling in structures such as these, the Israelites were to reflect that they were "strangers and sojourners" and that God had made the children of Israel to dwell in booths when He brought them out of the land of Egypt (Lev. 23.43). In their pleasant arboreal dwellings, they also had ample time to rejoice and to look forward to the gladness that would accompany the celebration of the feast in Jerusalem in the Age to Come, as described in Zechariah 14.16–19.

In Leviticus 23.40, four species of trees are mentioned in the commandment for the Feast of Tabernacles: "And ye shall take you on the first day the boughs (Hebrew—fruit) of goodly trees, branches of palm trees and the boughs

The lulav *used by Jews today is the same as that used in ancient times. The composition of the* lulav *is one palm branch, three myrtle twigs, two willow branches and one ethrog or citron.*

of thick trees and willows of the brook; and ye shall rejoice before the LORD your God seven days." Some sects, such as the Saduccees, believed this to be a list of materials from which the booths should be constructed. As we have seen, however, in the time of Nehemiah, trees other than those listed were used in the construction of the booths. The Pharisees, on the other hand, believed that the Four Kinds, as they were called, were to be carried in the hands of the celebrants of the feast. Certainly, in the time of Christ, they were used in this way. The Mishnaic tractate *Sukkah* gives the minute specifications necessary for choosing the four elements that were arranged in a bouquet and which were collectively known as a "*lulav*."

The "fruit of goodly trees" was identified with an ethrog or citron fruit, and the "boughs of thick trees" as myrtle twigs. A palm branch and willow branches completed the bouquet, with various proportions of each stipulated by different rabbis.

The scenes in the marketplaces in the Jerusalem of Christ's day can hardly have differed from those in present-day Jerusalem with the heads of the families carefully examining each of the four elements that make up the *lulav* and checking ethrogs for blemishes that would spoil their validity in the days preceding the feast. When the people met Jesus riding on an ass into Jerusalem, they greeted him with palm branches identical to those that formed part of the *lulav*.

Apart from the dwelling in booths there were distinctive sacrifices associated with the festival. Numbers 29.12–40 enumerates the offerings for the first day of the feast and the following six days, each of which had their own offerings. Each day, the burnt offerings consisted of fourteen lambs of the first year without blemish, two rams and one he-goat, with their corresponding meal- and drink-offerings. In addition there was an offering of bullocks, whose number decreased every day, so that on the first day of the feast,

thirteen bullocks were offered, while on the last day only seven. On the eighth day or octave on the day following, a single bullock was offered. Edersheim computed the total number of each type of sacrifice, noting that each was divisible by seven. He reckoned that "we have for the week 70 bullocks, 14 rams and 98 lambs, or altogether 182 sacrifices (26 x 7), to which must be added 336 (48 x 7) tenths of ephahs of flour for the meat (meal) offering." He writes that "whereas the sacred number 7 appeared at the Feast of Unleavened Bread only in the number of its days, and at Pentecost in the period of its observance (7 x 7 days after Passover), the Feast of Tabernacles lasted seven days, took place when the seventh month was at its full height and had the number 7 impressed on its characteristic sacrifices" (p. 240).

Associated with the offerings was a daily ceremonial of water-drawing. Early in the morning, on the 15th of *Tishrei*, a priest and a procession of others, among them musicians, went down to the Pool of Siloam. There the priest filled a golden flagon with water and the group filed back up to the Temple Mount. The priest would then make his way to the Altar to complete the water libation.

After drawing water from the Pool of Siloam, the priest and his procession would return to the Temple Mount, crossing the platform just before other priests climbed the Altar to lay the pieces of the morning sacrifice. As he arrived at the Water Gate, just to the right of that part of the Temple complex shown here, the priest was greeted by three trumpet blasts on his way to the Altar to complete the water libation ceremony.

The water-libation ceremony. The priest who carried the flagon of water was joined on the Altar by another priest who carried the wine of the drink-offering. There were two silver bowls, one on the west side of the Altar for the water and one on the east for the wine. The bowls were perforated on the bottom to allow the liquid to flow (most probably through pipes) down the brook of Kedron, the bowl for the wine having a wider hole as wine flows more slowly than water. Simultaneously, the priests poured their flagons into the two bowls with the people urging the priests "Lift up thine hand" (Sukkah *4.9) to make sure that the liquid was poured into the bowls and not onto the ground.*

The water-libation rite was performed daily during the Feast of Tabernacles. For the special circumstances of the Sabbath, the water was drawn from the Siloam Pool the previous evening and kept overnight in a special chamber. Once the libation had been made, the *Hallel* was sung to the accompaniment of music. In connection with this, the Mishnah records "And where do they shake the *lulav*? At the beginning and the end of the Psalm 'O give thanks unto the Lord' and at 'Save now, we beseech thee, O Lord'" (*Sukkah* 3.9). Knowing this we are struck at the inevitability of the multitude cutting down branches from the trees (palm trees) and strawing them in the way, using these very words: "Hosanna (Save now I beseech thee) to the Son of David. Blessed is he that cometh in the name of the Lord" (Matt. 21.8–9).

Jesus also used the water-libation to arrest the attention of his hearers as recorded in John's Gospel "in the last day, that great day of the feast" (7.37–38). Here Jesus points out the greatly superior nature of faith in him: "If any man thirst, let him come unto me and drink, He that believeth on me, as the Scripture hath said, out of his belly shall flow rivers of living water."

Associated with the water-drawing was one of the most picturesque rites of the Temple service. Known as the rejoicing over the water-drawing, or *Beit ha-Sho'eva* (literally: The place of the water-drawing), this ceremony took place on the evening of the first day of the Feast of Tabernacles and thereafter on the remaining days of the feast.

Towering golden lampstands which

were set up in the Court of the Women cast their light over the whole city. As *Sukkah* 5.3 puts it, "there was not a courtyard in Jerusalem that did not reflect the light of the *Beth ha-Sho'eva.*" Each lampstand had four bowls reached by four ladders, on which stood four youths of priestly families who filled the bowls with oil.

Pious men or *Hassidim* danced before the people with flaming torches while a Levitical choir stood on the fifteen steps chanting the Songs of Ascents and "countless" other Levites played music on various Temple instruments. The strong impression on the people made by this spectacular tableau must have been in the mind of Jesus when he uttered the words, "I am the light of the world" (John 8.12).

A golden lampstand in the Court of the Women during the rejoicing over the water-drawing.

The New Year

Blowing the trumpet or shofar *at the New Year. The* shofar *blowers (an Israeli soldier stands in center) have as their background the Western Wall in Jerusalem.*

After dealing with the three major festivals, Edersheim goes back in time to deal with the other two feasts of the seventh month—the New Year (or *Rosh ha-Shanah*) and the Day of Atonement (*Yom Kippur*). The New Year, or commencement of the civil year, began with the new moon or first day of the month of *Tishrei*. New moons were always celebrated by the Israelites since the commandment was received by Moses (Num. 28.11).

Strict accuracy in observing the new moons was necessary to ensure that the feasts were celebrated at the right time. In order to avoid disputes, Rabbi Gamaliel, mentioned as the teacher of Paul in Acts 22.3, is said to have kept a chart showing the phases of the moon in his upper chamber (*Rosh ha-Shanah* 2.8).

Scripture describes the New Year as "a sabbath, a memorial of blowing of trumpets, an holy convocation" (Lev. 23.24) and as "a day of blowing of trumpets" (Num. 29.1). This was because the blowing of trumpets or *shofars* was a major feature of the feast. However, the Mishnah makes it clear that it was not the usual silver trumpets that were used, but animal horns. In *Rosh ha-Shanah* 3.3–4 we are told that "The *shofar* blown in the Temple at the New Year was made from the horn of the wild goat, straight, with its mouthpiece overlaid with gold. . . . The *shofars* on days of fasting were ram's horns, rounded, with their mouthpiece overlaid with silver." The use of such horns was meant to recall the sacrifice of Isaac, when a ram with curved horns took the place of Isaac on the altar.

Apart from the *shofar* blowing, the only other injunction for New Year's Day was the offering of sacrifices. These comprised a special festive offering of a young bullock, a ram and seven lambs, in addition to the usual morning and evening sacrifices and the burnt offering of the regular new moon.

There is no record of Jesus taking part in the New Year's Day ritual in the Temple, as the day could also be celebrated in any of the synagogues around the country. However, towards the end of his life, he spent more time in Jerusalem, and would surely have taken part in this "feast of blowing of trumpets" in the vicinity of the Temple.

The Day of Atonement

(overleaf) The High Priest in the Holy of Holies on the Day of Atonement.

The ten days between *Rosh ha-Shanah* and the Day of Atonement was a period of penitence in preparation for the most solemn day in the Jewish calendar. The Scriptural injunction then, for the 10th of *Tishrei*, was that "it shall be an holy convocation unto you; and ye shall afflict your souls, and offer an offering made by fire unto the LORD.

"And ye shall do no work in that same day: for it is a day of atonement, to make an atonement for you before the LORD your God.

"For whatsoever soul it be that shall not be afflicted in that same day, he shall be cut off from among his people" (Lev. 23.27–29).

As Edersheim points out, "it took place on the tenth day of the seventh month (*Tishrei*), that is, symbolically, when the sacred or Sabbath of the months had just attained its completeness" (p. 265). It was also unique in that it was the High Priest and not the ordinary priests that officiated. Another unique feature was that the worshippers were commanded to fast for the twenty-four hours of the feast (or at least that is how they interpreted the injunction "ye shall afflict your souls"). The sacrifices were also on a much greater propitiatory scale involving, as Maimonides, the twelfth-century Jewish sage, observed, the sacrifice of fifteen different animals.

The most solemn part of the day's service was the entrance into the Holy of Holies by the High Priest. This is the event referred to by the apostle Paul in his letter to the Hebrews 9.7: "But into the second (the Holy of Holies) went the High Priest alone once every year, not without blood, which he offered for himself and for the errors of the people." The Mishnaic tractate *Yoma* records how strictly the High Priest was prepared for this solemnity. This was all the more important as the office of the High Priesthood had, during the time of Christ, deteriorated, with cases of nepotism, deviation from the strict marriage laws and a poor knowledge of the Scriptures being rife among the holders of the office. The High Priest was taken from his home into a special chamber in the Temple seven days before the feast and during the week he practiced the rites he would have to perform on the great day itself. Due to the awe in which this ceremony was held, a substitute priest was chosen in case anything should happen to the High Priest himself.

When the day arrived, the ritual had to be performed in strict order as recorded in the Mishnah. "Every act (of the High Priest) on the Day of Atonement here enumerated according to the prescribed order—if one act was done (out of order) before another act, it is as if it was not done at all" (*Yoma* 5.7).

For this occasion the High Priest is dressed not in his usual brightly colored garments but in white robes. He would change his clothes five times throughout the day, immersing himself in water each time. In the morning, he wore linen of Pelusium and in the afternoon, Indian linen. After offering the morning sacrifice, he would confess his sins over the bullock that was destined for the sin-offering. Next he chose the scapegoat from among two goats and presented it before the people. He then returned to the Sanctuary again and laid his hands upon the bullock, this time confessing the sin for "the seed of Aaron, thy holy people." His next action was to kill the bullock, catch

his blood in a basin and hand it to another priest to stir so as to prevent it from coagulating.

Then the great moment arrived. From the Altar of Burnt Offering, the High Priest took burning coals on his fire-pan and with a ladle carrying two handfuls of incense, entered into the Sanctuary. He made his way through the double curtain which separated the Holy from the Holy of Holies to offer this incense. Under Mosaic Law and in the time of the Ark of the Covenant, the incense was burnt before the mercy-seat of the Ark. With the absence of the Ark in the Second Temple, the incense censer was placed on what was called the Foundation Stone, as we learn from *Yoma* 5.2: "After the Ark was taken away one stone remained there from the time of the early prophets, and it was called *Shetiyah* (Foundation). It was higher than the ground than three fingerbreadths. On this he used to put (the fire-pan)."

Outside, the worshippers awaited anxiously for the High Priest to emerge, and so he was under a strict injunction not to prolong his prayer. When he came out he took the blood of the bullock and again entered the Holy Place, sprinkling the blood in the stipulated manner towards the former site of the mercy-seat. He then killed the sin offering—the goat that had not been chosen to be the scapegoat—and entered the Holy of Holies for the third time that day with its blood, which he again sprinkled according to the strict laws of the service. He also cleansed with the blood, the Veil, the Holy Place, the Altar of Incense and the Altar of Burnt Offering. But, as Edersheim puts it, "The consciences were not free from a sense of personal guilt and sin. That remained to be done through the 'scape-goat'" (p. 277).

The choosing of the scapegoat took place on the north side of the Altar. The High Priest came and stood there, flanked by the priest that was next in rank (and officially his substitute) and the chief priest of the course for the day. Two he-goats were brought and presented, in the words of Leviticus 16.7, "before the LORD at the door of the tabernacle of the congregation." There was also what the Mishnah calls a "casket" (*Yoma* 3.9) which Edersheim translates "an urn" (Hebrew, *Calpi*) (p. 272) containing two lots, one with the inscription "For the Lord" (*Yahweh*) and the other "For *Azazel*" (the scapegoat). The High Priest faced the people, shook the *Calpi* and took out two lots, laying one on the head of each goat. A thread of crimson wool was tied to the head of the goat that was chosen to be the scapegoat, while a similar thread was tied around the throat of the goat which was for the Lord, signifying that he was to be slaughtered. The scapegoat was then turned round to face the people. As Edersheim writes, "assuredly a more marked type of Christ could not be conceived as he was brought forth by Pilate and stood before the people, just as He was about

To choose the scapegoat on the Day of Atonement, two he-goats were brought "before the LORD at the door of the tabernacle of the congregation" (Lev. 16.7)—one "for the Lord" and the other "for Azazel*" (the scapegoat).*

to be led forth, bearing the iniquity of the people" (p. 273).

Following the presentation of the scapegoat, the High Priest returned to the Sanctuary to confess his sins over the bullock. The scapegoat was kept, standing facing the people until the ritual of the slaughter of the bullock and the entry of the High Priest into the Holy of Holies had been enacted. After the cleansing of the Sanctuary, the focus moved back to the scapegoat for the performance of a strange ritual unique to the Day of Atonement.

Reaching the scapegoat, the High Priest laid his hands on its head and confessed over it the sins of Israel. Then the priests led the scapegoat, to which the sins of the people had been symbolically transferred, toward the gate in the eastern wall, through which it was brought out via a bridge over to the Mount of Olives. From here the scapegoat was led to the wilderness, unto a precipice that tradition holds was 90 *ris* (12 miles) from Jerusalem. The journey was divided into equidistant portions, none more than a Sabbath day's journey. Finally, a "fit man" (Hebrew, "man of opportunity") went alone with the scapegoat to the precipice, where he pushed him over the edge to fall to his death. This killing of the scapegoat was not according to Mosaic ordinance but a rabbinic injunction. Scripture stipulates only that he be let go into the wilderness. Its arrival in the wilderness was signalled to the Temple, where the people rejoiced that the scapegoat had borne their sins away to "a land not inhabited" (Hebrew, "a land cut off") (Lev. 16.22).

The meaning of this strange ritual is wonderfully explained by Edersheim (p. 284) as pointing toward "the final, real and complete removal of sin by the Lord Jesus Christ as we read in Isaiah 53.6—'Jehovah (*Yahweh*) hath made the iniquity of us all to meet on him.'"

But the service did not end there. While the scapegoat was being led away, the High Priest took the carcasses of the bullock and the he-goat, cut them open, took away the sacrificial portions and had their bodies burnt. The High Priest was then given the scroll of the Law, from which he read certain passages relating to the Day of Atonement. This being completed, the High Priest again washed and changed into his golden vestments and proceeded to offer a goat for the sin offering, burnt offerings for both himself and for the people and the inner parts of the bullock and goat. His day's work ended with the offering of the daily evening sacrifice and accompanying ritual. The friends of the High Priest accompanied him to his house, where a feast was held to honor his safe deliverance from the Holy of Holies.

The Feast of Purim

The Scroll of Esther.

Purim is the first of the post-Mosaic festivals, those festivals that were not mentioned in the Law of Moses but which entered into the calendar of the Jews to commemorate some great national event.

The feast of Purim or Lots, which takes place on the 14th and 15th of *Adar* (usually in March), commemorates the deliverance of the Jews in Persia by Jewish Queen Esther from the wicked Haman. According to the Book of Esther, the feast is to be "a day of gladness and feasting and a good day and of sending portions one to another" (9.19). They were also enjoined in the Book of Esther that "the memorial of them should not perish from their seed" (9.28). This is done through the public reading of the Scroll or *Megillah* of Esther on the 14th of *Adar* and on the following day. In walled cities, such as Jerusalem, the festival is celebrated a day later, to commemorate the way in which the Jews in the walled capital of Shushan celebrated the Festival on the 15th of *Adar*, having had to defend themselves against their enemies on the 14th.

A special Mishnaic tractate called *Megillah* was written stipulating the time and manner of the public reading of the Scroll of Esther during the Feast of Purim, as well as that of other parts of Scripture at different times. Jesus would doubtless have heard this read, as a reference in Scripture makes it clear that he came up to Jerusalem during this feast. Following chapter 4 of John, in which Jesus had pronounced that harvest was four months away, indicating that the time in which he was speaking was December, it is written, "After this there was a feast of the Jews: and Jesus went up to Jerusalem" (John 5.1). As the next reference to the time of year in the narrative is to the Feast of Passover (John 6.4), the allusion in chapter 5.1 must be to the Feast of Purim, an argument made by Edersheim (pp. 290–291).

During the first century, the ceremonial of the feast appears to have comprised the observance of the Fast of Esther on the day the scroll was read, the public reading of the scroll, and sending one another gifts of food. The carnival atmosphere of Purim today is a modern innovation. Children of religious families dress in costumes of biblical heroes while their secular counterparts masquerade as the latest cartoon characters or pop idols. During the public reading of the scroll, a din is created with rattles whenever Haman's name is mentioned so as to bring as much indignity as possible on the defeated oppressor.

The Feast of Hanukkah

The next feast of commemoration to be instituted was the feast of Hanukkah or Dedication. This was celebrated in memory of the rededication of the Temple in 164 B.C. after its desecration by another oppressor of the Jews, the Syro-Greek Antiochus Epiphanes. The date of its observance is the 25th of *Kislev*, which corresponds to December. There is a clear reference to the participation of Jesus in this feast in the Gospel of John 10.22–23. Here it is written: "And it was at Jerusalem the feast of the dedication and it was winter. And Jesus walked in the temple in Solomon's Porch."

Solomon's Porch is identified with the eastern portico of the Temple Mount. The eastern wall was the only side of the Herodian Temple that followed the same line as the Temple of Solomon, for the simple reason that because of the sheer drop into the Kedron Valley, the platform could not be extended on this side. At this time of year the colonnade, built mainly to provide shade from the fierce summer sun, gave shelter from the winter elements. It was the backdrop to an exchange between Jesus and the Pharisees. Reading the Gospel of John, we can imagine the scene—Jesus taking the opportunity to walk quietly in the portico named after his ancestor, being surrounded by the Pharisees, demanding that he reveal whether or not he was the awaited Messiah. His answer, "the works that I do in my Father's name, they bear witness of me . . . I and my father are one" (John 10.25, 10.30), the Pharisees regarded as blasphemous. There must have been a supply of stones in the area as, with stones in their hand, they threatened to stone him. However, as the gospel record puts it, "he escaped out of their hand" (v. 39).

The feast was also known as the Festival of Lights, because of the lighting of an eight-branched lampstand in commemoration of the miracle which took place in the Temple in 164 B.C. This miracle is recounted in the apocryphal Book of Maccabees 2. The Maccabees were a family from Modiin, a village to the west of Jerusalem. In response to the defilement of the Temple by Antiochus, when he cooked a pig in the Temple and poured its

broth on the altar and then tried to enforce the sacrifice of pigs in their village, the Maccabees revolted against the Syrians. Judah the Maccabee led the Jews to victory, captured the Temple, and re-dedicated it on the 25th of *Kislev*. However, when the oil for the lighting of the golden Lampstand was discovered, there was found enough oil only for one day. The Book of Maccabees records that the oil miraculously lasted for a full eight days, when new supplies arrived.

Today, Hanukkah is celebrated using a special eight-branched candlestick or *Hanukkiah*. On the first night of Hanukkah, the family gathers round the *Hanukkiah* as the first candle is lit with the *Shamash* (or extra attendant light). On the second night, two candles are lit. Then working left to right, three, then four, until by the eighth night, all eight are burning. It is a joyful family festival. To remind the Jews of the miracle of the oil, many of the special foods eaten during the eight days are prepared with oil, such as potato pancakes and doughnuts.

Solomon's Porch, the eastern portico of the Temple Mount (facing the Temple and above the eastern wall).

The Sacrifice of the Red Heifer

Edersheim calls the purification of the Red Heifer "a service distinguished from the rest by its unique character" (p. 301). He compares this with the purification after the birth of a first-born son, which Mary undertook in the Temple following the birth of Jesus. The latter service was not nearly as solemn as that required on defilement from contact with death.

For cases such as these and of course, individuals would regularly come into contact with the dead, the Mosaic Law contained the following injunction: "But the man that shall be unclean and shall not purify himself, that soul shall be cut off from among his congregation, because he hath defiled the sanctuary of the LORD: the water of separation hath not been sprinkled upon him; he is unclean" (Num. 19.20).

This "water of separation" (or "rejection" as it is in Hebrew) was water mixed with a substance that was prepared under conditions so rare that it is reckoned to have been prepared only about seven times from the time of Moses to the destruction of the Temple in A.D. 70. This substance was the ashes of a red heifer which, according to Scripture, had to be "without spot, wherein is no blemish and upon which never came yoke" (Num. 19.2). However, in *Parah*, the Mishnaic tractate devoted to the subject of the Red Heifer, the Rabbis stipulate how stringently the requirements that the heifer be completely red in color had to be met: "If it had two black or white hairs growing from within a single hole it is invalid" (2.5).

In order to obtain the ashes from the Red Heifer, the priest chosen to burn the animal, sometimes the High Priest himself, was kept for seven days in a

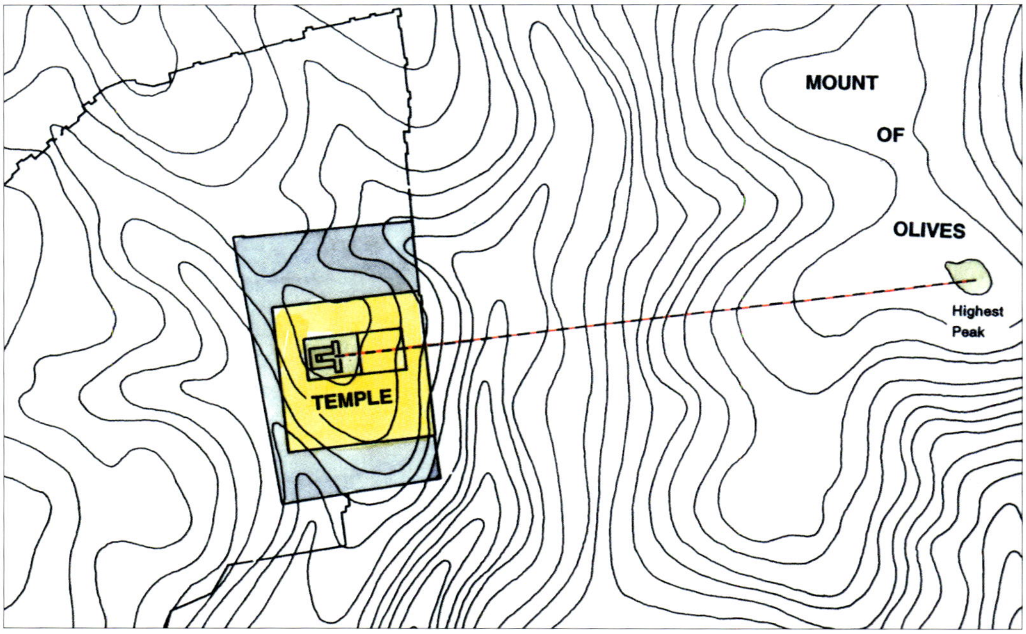

The sacrifice of the Red Heifer. This map shows the line of vision from the door of the Sanctuary to the top of the Mount of Olives. It makes it clear that if this location of the Temple is accepted, the stipulation regarding the sprinkling of the blood of the Red Heifer towards the Holy of Holies from the Mount of Olives could be met.

special chamber deep inside the Temple. During this period, the priest, with the heifer, passed in procession over an arched bridge leading from the eastern gate of the Temple up to the Mount of Olives. The bridge was designed in this way so that any impurity from the graves that may have lain underneath could not pass through. After immersing himself in a ritual bath, the priest slaughtered the red heifer which had been tied to a pile of cedar, pine, spruce and fig-tree wood. Next the priest had to catch the blood of the heifer and sprinkle it seven times toward the Holy of Holies (the Tabernacle in ancient times). After this, the wood was lit and the burnt remains of the heifer were beaten and sieved into ashes. These ashes were divided into three portions: one was kept on the Temple Terrace (*Hel*), a second on the Mount of Olives, and the third was shared among the priests for use in their own localities.

We do not know if a Red Heifer was actually sacrificed during the lifetime of Christ, but it is certain that he saw and heard many times of purifications from defilements by the dead by the ashes of a red heifer.

Today, some Jews in Israel are looking for such a red heifer in order to purify themselves so that the Temple can be built and redemption obtained.

Purification from Leprosy

Edersheim deals next with the purification of the leper. It is this that Jesus refers to when he says to the cleansed leper, "Go thy way, shew thyself to the priest, and offer the gift that Moses commanded for a testimony unto them" (Matt. 8.4).

Lepers were among the most despised members of the community in all of Israel. Indeed, they were not really part of the community as long as they were leprous. "All the days wherein the plague shall be in him he shall be defiled; he is unclean; he shall dwell alone; without the camp shall his habitation be" (Lev. 13.46).

The offering of two sparrows was used to cleanse oneself of leprosy.

The Mishnah has a particularly long tractate called *Negaim*, which elaborates on the instructions for examination of leprosy signs given in Leviticus 13. The final chapter of tractate *Negaim*, chapter 14, also elaborates on the ceremony of the cleansing of the leper as recorded in Scripture (Leviticus 14). Two living clean birds (probably sparrows) were brought with cedar wood, scarlet and hyssop. The priest killed one of the birds in an earthenware vessel over running water. The bird that was kept alive was then dipped in the blood of its fellow, together with the cedar wood, scarlet and hyssop. The healed leper was then sprinkled with the blood while the living bird was released. Then the leper had to wash his clothes, shave off all his hair and wash in water before being allowed into the camp (or into a walled city in post-Mosaic times). However, for seven days he was not allowed to enter his own home or to have marital relations. On the eighth day, he had to bring one he-lamb for a trespass offering, another he-lamb for a burnt offering, and a ewe-lamb for a sin offering. A unique feature of this offering was that the priest had to put the blood of the trespass offering on the tip of the leper's right ear, the thumb of his right hand and the big toe of his right foot (all places that signified executive actions).

(overleaf) A woman suspected of adultery (the figure in black, in front of the gate) undergoing purification at the Nicanor Gate.

(opposite page) Artist's reconstruction of the offering from the Nazarite upon the completion of his vow. He is shown in the Chamber of the Nazarite, in the southeast corner of the Court of the Women, where he is boiling the flesh of his peace offerings in a cauldron,

In Mosaic times, this was done before the door of the Tabernacle. In the Second Temple period, however, the leper went to the Gate of Nicanor after bathing in the Chamber of the Lepers. The leper then thrust his hand into the Temple Court, which he was not yet allowed to enter, while the priest performed the above ritual. The priest took and sprinkled some of the log of oil, which the leper had to bring with his offering of three measures of fine flour, seven times toward the Holy of Holies. He then put the oil on the same parts of the leper's body where he had put the blood. The remainder of the oil was poured over the leper's head for atonement. The sin offering and the burnt offering were then offered on the altar, after which the leper was considered to be fully cleansed from his defilement.

Jesus must have seen many lepers in his lifetime. The first part of the ceremony, with the bird being set free in the open field, could be performed anywhere. The part which took place after the interval of seven days must have been a regular occurrence in the Temple. The poignant picture of the leper longingly putting his hand into the Temple Court from which he was still barred must have stayed in the mind of Christ, with the knowledge that the bird that was killed and the bird that was set free, both pointed toward himself.

Purification from Adultery

Another purification rite, which took place at the Nicanor Gate of the Temple, was for the woman suspected of adultery. She was brought to this place to perform the rite which, in the time of Moses, took place simply "before the LORD" (Num. 5.16), that is, in front of the Tabernacle. The Mishnah, in a tractate entitled *Sotah* ("The suspected adulteress"), adds much to the original stipulations of Numbers 5. Edersheim's footnote is apposite: "The tractate *Sotah* enters into every possible detail, with prurient casuistry—the testimony always in Jewish criminal law being in favour of the accused" (p. 319).

From *Sotah* 1.1, we understand that a wife suspected of adultery could only be brought to trial if she had been previously warned by her husband before two witnesses, whereas in Numbers 5 the husband's "spirit of jealousy" (v. 14) alone is reason to bring the suspected wife to trial. The Mishnah stipulates that, after being brought to the Nicanor Gate, the woman's upper garments are torn so that her bosom is exposed to all, to her shame. The situation is handled with far more propriety and less cruelty in the Scriptural injunction: "And the priest shall set the woman before the LORD and uncover the woman's head, which is the jealousy offering" (Num. 5.18). In this way, shame is brought on the woman by laying bare only her head.

The two accounts then overlap as the priest in the Mishnaic description reads a specially written scroll containing Numbers 5.19–22, which details the priest's charge that if she was unfaithful, the water she was to be given would cause her "thigh to rot" and her "belly to swell." This water was given to her in an earthenware vessel. Dust from the floor of the tabernacle (in pre-Temple times) or from the Temple floor was sprinkled on the water. She also offered an offering of a tenth part of an *ephah* of barley meal. In the Scriptural account she first makes her offering and then drinks the bitter water.

If guilty, she was expected to exhibit signs of illness straight away. In Rabbinic times, it was believed that "merit," which the woman may have earned in the past, could delay the onset of symptoms. If she was innocent, it would be obvious for all to see.

The Nazarite Vow

The completion of the Nazarite vow was another rite that brought pilgrims to the Temple. Great caution in the taking of vows was advocated in the Law of Moses: "If a man vow a vow unto the LORD, or swear an oath to bind his soul with a bond, he shall not break his word, he shall do according to all that proceedeth out of his mouth" (Num. 30.2).

A vow made it possible for an Israelite to give himself to God for a stipulated time and so could not be made lightly. As Edersheim points out (p. 326), the Vow of the Nazarite was a vow of separation (the word "*nezer*" is derived from the root "*nazar*" which means "to separate"). Again, an entire Mishnaic tractate, *Nazir*, is devoted to the subject. In passage 6.1, the obligations of this vow are summarized: "Three things are forbidden to the Nazarite: uncleanness, cutting off the hair, and aught that comes from the vine." He was to avoid all defilement with the dead, including his closest family members. He was to let his hair grow, and abstain from wine, grapes, raisins or anything derived from the vine. (Examples of Nazarites in the Scriptures were Samson, Samuel and John the Baptist.)

The vow itself could be made in any place and even an approximation of the words used in making the vow were regarded as though the vow had indeed been made. However, the conclusion of the vow (for those vows that were made for a certain duration with a stipulated minimum of thirty-one days—some Nazarites became such for the remainder of their life) necessitated a visit to the Temple, as under the Law, presentation at the door of the Tabernacle would have been mandatory.

The Nazarite had to bring a lamb for a burnt offering, a ewe-lamb for a sin offering and a ram for a peace offering.

The firstfruits were presented in baskets. The rich brought their offering in baskets overlaid with silver and gold. The poor used simple baskets made of willow branches.

All the sacrifices had to be unblemished. With these he brought a basket of unleavened loaves of bread and wafers with their meal and drink offerings. These were offered through the priest, after which the Nazarite went to the Chamber of the Nazarite in the southeast corner of the Court of the Women.

Here, after having boiled the flesh of his peace offerings in a cauldron over a fire, he would shave off his long hair and toss it into the fire. The priest would then wave the offering before God, after which the Nazarite was free from his vow of separation and could again drink wine.

This vow was certainly observed in the time of Christ and for some years afterward. See the reference to Paul supporting and identifying with four Nazarites in the Book of Acts 21.23–26.

Offering of the Firstfruits

Apart from the national firstfruit offering of the *Omer* at Passover and the two wave-loaves in the Feast of Weeks, Israelites were enjoined to offer their own firstfruits, "The first of the firstfruits of thy land thou shalt bring into the house of the LORD thy God" (Ex. 23.19). Again, this rite could only be performed when the Temple stood. The Mishnaic tractate devoted to the subject, *Bikkurim* (firstfruits), stipulates that they be brought after the Feast of Weeks. In practice they were brought sometime between this feast and the 25th of *Kislev*, or Dedication of the Temple. It also states that they be brought only from the "seven kinds" for which the land was known, which are enumerated in Deuteronomy 8.8: wheat, barley, grapes, figs, pomegranates, olives and dates.

It must have been a very joyous occasion when the farmer would choose what he would bring to the Temple to offer to the Lord. The Mishnah describes how he would go down to his field and tie a piece of reed-grass round the first ripe fig or other fruit and say, "Lo, these are First-fruits" (*Bikkurim* 3.1). One can imagine him explaining to his children that these were the fruits of the land which God had given them.

As Edersheim writes, "then he renewed his covenant relationship to God each year as 'the winter was past, the rain over and gone, the flowers appeared on the earth, the time of the singing of birds was come and the voice of the turtle was heard in the land, the fig-tree put forth his green figs and the vines with the tender grapes gave a good smell' (Song 2.11–13). And as these fruits gradually ripened, the ceremonies connected first with setting them apart and then with offering them, must have continued in every Israelitish household during the greater portion of the year, from early spring till winter" (pp. 336–337).

The way in which the firstfruits were brought to the Temple was also replete with interest. Not all Israelites could bring up their offerings personally. Instead, they sent representatives or "stationary men" from the various regions of the Land up to Jerusalem with those who could journey there themselves. They first assembled in a central location in their area, camped outdoors, an essential part of the ritual, until they heard the wake-up call "arise and let us go up to Zion unto the Lord our God," taken from Jeremiah 31.6.

The procession through the Land must have been a lovely sight. Those that lived far from Jerusalem brought dried fruits in their baskets while those that lived near enough brought fresh produce. The band of pilgrims followed an ox that would eventually become a peace offering. The horns of the ox were overlaid with gold and decorated with olive leaves. The music of the flute led them onward until they reached Jerusalem, where the company was greeted by the rulers of the Temple in accordance with the importance of the place from whence they came. When they reached the Temple Mount, each pilgrim would take his basket, which had been put in its final arrangement before entering Jerusalem, upon his shoulder and enter as far as the Temple Court.

With basket on shoulder, each in turn recited from the avowal in Deuteronomy 26, beginning at verse 3, "I profess this day unto the LORD thy God, that I am come unto the country which the LORD sware unto our fathers for to give us...a Syrian ready to perish was my father . . ." and concluding with verse 10: "And now, behold, I have brought the firstfruits of the land, which thou, O LORD, hast given me. And thou shalt set it before the LORD thy God, and worship before the LORD thy God."

The priest then put his hand under the basket and waved it before God. After concluding the saying of his avowal, he left his basket beside the Altar. The pilgrims were expected to be able to recite the avowal but those that could not, repeated the words after the priest. The Mishnah makes the interesting observation that because some felt humiliated by this practice, everyone, even those who knew the words, were enjoined to recite after the priest! The firstfruits then became the property of the priests, part of the offerings that sustained them, in the spirit of the Scripture, "the LORD is their inheritance" (Deut. 10.9).

(overleaf) Company of pilgrims bringing their firstfruits to the Temple in Jerusalem.

The Hope of Rebuilding the Temple

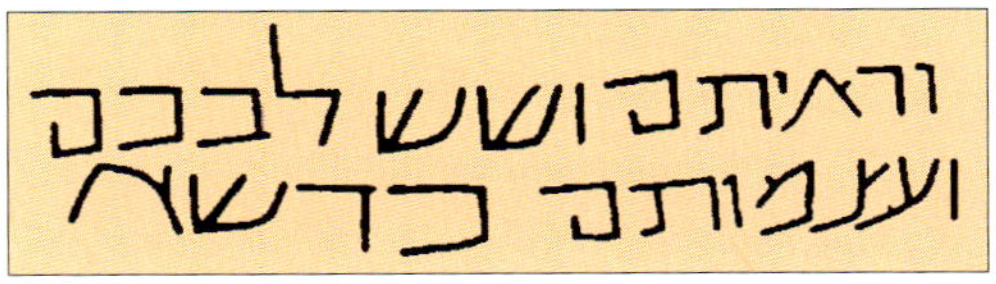

Inscription showing the hope of the Jews to rebuild the Temple. It is thought to date from the time of Emperor Julian the Apostate (361–363).

The inscription is a quotation from Isaiah 66.4:

וראיתם ושש לבבכם
ועצמותם כדשא

U-ra-ee-tem ve-sas lib-chem ve-atzmotam ka-deshe

"And when ye shall see this your heart shall rejoice and your bones shall flourish as the herb."

In the inscription, "your bones" is changed to "their bones" and is presumed to refer to those of the dead about to be resurrected.

Edersheim concludes his preface with the words: "As I proceeded, the conviction has always been deepened that Christ is indeed 'the end of the Law for righteousness,' to whom all the ordinances of the Old Testament had pointed and in whom alone, alike the people and the history of Israel find their meaning. Viewed in this light, the Temple services are not so many strange or isolated rites, for the origin of which we must look among neighbouring nations, or in the tendencies natural to men during the infancy of their history. Rather, all now becomes one connected whole—the design and execution bearing even stronger evidence to its Divine authorship than other of God's works" (p. xi).

With its destruction in A.D. 70, the ritual associated with the Temple could no longer be observed. It would appear that in the years closely following the destruction, some remains of the Temple could still be seen. The Babylonian Talmud records that Rabbi Akiva, standing on Mount Scopus with other sages, saw a jackal emerge from the rubble of the Holy of Holies. With the ascent to power of the Emperor Hadrian in A.D. 117, the Jews were hopeful that they could rebuild the Temple but their hopes were dashed when, in A.D. 129, he came to Jerusalem to begin the erection of a Roman colony on the ruins of the city.

In A.D. 132, the Jewish leader Simeon Bar Kokhba ("Son of a Star"), who was looked upon as a Messiah, led his people in revolt. A coin found from this period which depicts the facade of the Temple indicates to some scholars that he actually rebuilt the Temple. He did restore the priesthood and began a new calendar system. If the Temple was indeed rebuilt at this time, we have no record of it other than the aforementioned coin which may, in fact, have depicted an idealized Temple.

During the Byzantine period the site was as desolate as in Roman times. The Roman Emperor Julian the Apostate acceded to the throne in 361, and although educated as a Christian, he reacted against what he saw as the persecution of other beliefs. Julian issued an edict of universal toleration and announced in 363 that he would rebuild the Temple in Jerusalem.

However, during the construction of the new Temple, some catastrophe apparently caused the work to stop. This may have been the earthquake which also destroyed the city of Petra.

Throughout the centuries, with the successive appropriation of the Temple site by Muslims, Crusaders and Turks, the Jews never lost hope of restoring the Temple and its sacrifices. In this generation, the Temple Institute in the Jewish Quarter of the Old City of Jerusalem is devoted to the reconstruction of the Temple vessels according to historical and archaeological sources.